Twayne's United States Authors Series

EDITOR OF THIS VOLUME

Sylvia E. Bowman
Indiana University

John Hay

TUSAS 296

Courtesy of Brown University Library

John Hay

JOHN HAY

By ROBERT L. GALE
University of Pittsburgh

TWAYNE PUBLISHERS
A DIVISION OF G. K. HALL & CO., BOSTON

Library of Congress Cataloging in Publication Data

Gale, Robert L.
    John Hay.

    (Twayne's United States authors series; TUSAS 296)

    Bibliography: p. 147 - 55
    Includes index.
    1.   Hay, John, 1838 - 1905.   2.   Authors, American
— 19th century—Biography.   3.   Statesmen—United
States—Biography.
PS1903.G3   818'.4'09   77-27650
ISBN 0-8057-7199-9

To Maureen
Here's to making Hay

Contents

About the Author

Robert Lee Gale, who was born in Des Moines, Iowa, in 1919, was educated at Dartmouth College (B.A. 1942, *summa cum laude;* Phi Beta Kappa) and at Columbia University (M.A. 1947, Ph.D. 1952), where the late Lionel Trilling directed his dissertation on Henry James. Gale served in the U.S. Army Counter-Intelligence Corps in Europe during World War II. He has taught at Columbia University, the University of Delaware, the University of Mississippi, and the University of Pittsburgh (since 1959), where he is now Professor of American Literature. He has had Fulbright teaching fellowships to Italy and Finland, and has also lectured in Canada, Germany, Denmark, and Russia. He is the author of *The Caught Image: Figurative Language in the Fiction of Henry James; Thomas Crawford, American Sculptor; Plots and Characters in Henry James, Nathaniel Hawthorne, Herman Melville, Edgar Allan Poe*, and *Mark Twain;* the "Henry James" chapter in *Eight American Authors* (revised edition); and ten study guides on Henry David Thoreau, Stephen Crane, Ralph Waldo Emerson, Henry James, John Steinbeck, Theodore Dreiser, Edgar Allan Poe, and Edith Wharton. He had also contributed more than eighty essays and reviews to scholarly journals. In addition, Gale is the author of the TUSAS volumes on *Richard Henry Dana, Jr.,* and *Francis Parkman.* He is currently editing the Archon *Plots and Characters Series,* which will number about ten volumes in addition to those he has already written. He teaches courses and seminars in composition, nineteenth-century American fiction, Civil War literature, the American 1890s, Western American ("cowboy") literature, and the Roaring Twenties; he also teaches in adult-education and penitentiary study programs. He is married, and he and his wife have two sons and a daughter.

Preface

Although several books have discussed John Hay (1835 - 1905) as a statesman and as a friend of the illustrious, the present study is the first book to concentrate upon Hay as a man of letters. Chapters 1 - 3 discuss Hay's life. Chapter 1 deals with his boyhood, his education, his service as Abraham Lincoln's assistant private secretary, his legation work abroad, his editorial work on the New York *Tribune*, his marriage, his curious vacillation, and his writing of Lincoln's biography. Chapter 2 concerns not only his resumed dilettantism but also his work in the field of diplomacy—first as an ambassador to England and then as secretary of state under President William McKinley and President Theodore Roosevelt. Chapter 3 treats Hay's literary friendships with Henry Adams, Mark Twain, William Dean Howells, Henry James, and others.

In Chapters 4 - 8, I concentrate on Hay's varied writings. Chapter 4 treats his poetry, with emphasis on his popular *Pike County Ballads*. Chapter 5 is devoted to his *Castilian Days*, the literary consequence of his year's residence in Spain. Chapter 6 analyzes his fiction—his five short stories and the controversial, anonymously published, procapitalist novel *The Bread-Winners*. Chapter 7 discusses in considerable detail *Abraham Lincoln: A History*, the ten-volume collaboration of John G. Nicolay (Lincoln's other private secretary) and John Hay. In this discussion are treated its sources; its volume-by-volume organization; its authors' three main themes (war and politics as Siamese twins, fatalism, and humor as a saving grace); and finally its style. Chapter 8 handles Hay's major public addresses and then offers a brief summation.

One conclusion quickly emerges: Hay was a brilliant, erratic, amiable, dyspeptic, ultimately negative and self-deprecating literary genius for whom successes came easily to be rather despised. Another conclusion is that although his personality may well be insoluble, he was one of the most fascinating public and literary figures America has yet produced; he deserves to be better known and more generally respected. His dialect poetry is still pleasant; his book on Spain has vivid, worthwhile moments; and some of his fiction anticipates that of Henry James, William Dean Howells, Hamlin Garland, Theodore Dreiser, and Sherwood Anderson. His work on Lincoln is enduringly poignant. His modernity as secretary of state is still a hotly discussed issue in American diplomatic history. And many of his letters and diary entries, though not his usually vapid speeches, are sprightly, witty, informative, and bracing.

It is a pleasure to express my gratitude to persons and groups of aid to me in this work. George Monteiro of Brown University unstintingly shared with me his extensive knowledge of John Hay and related literary figures; and Stuart C. Sherman, librarian of the fabulous John Hay Library at Brown, generously showed me innumerable Hay treasures there. Roy P. Basler, chief of the Manuscripts Division, Reference Department, Library of Congress, Washington, D.C., and his associate Oliver H. Orr were most helpful. James W. Symington, Second District, Missouri, Congress of the United States, House of Representatives, told me much about his great-grandfather John Hay. Robert F. Metzdorf, library consultant, North Colebrook, Connecticut, gave me valuable suggestions. Bruce T. Hamilton, editorial assistant, Mark Twain Papers, University of California, Berkeley, provided the means to answer some questions concerning Hay's friendship with Twain (and I quote from Twain's writings by permission of Thomas G. Chamberlain and Manufacturers Hanover Trust Company as trustees under the Will of Clara Clemens Samossoud).

Rayburn S. Moore of the University of Georgia tried to help me locate the Hay half of the John Hay - Constance Fenimore Woolson correspondence, as did Kermit J. Pike, chief librarian, the Western Reserve Historical Society, Cleveland, Ohio. And the incomparable Alice Roosevelt Longworth gave me a memorable hour at tea time during an otherwise somber week in Washington, D.C. Staff members of libraries at the University of Pittsburgh, Carnegie-Mellon University, and Duquesne University, all in Pittsburgh, Pennsylvania, were efficient and generous. I am also grateful to the administrative officers of the University of Pittsburgh, especially Rhoten T. Smith, Jerome L. Rosenberg, Robert B. Hinman, and Walter H. Evert, for granting sabbaticial time and funds for travel. Once again, my gratitude to Sylvia E. Bowman, editor of the

Preface

Twayne United States Authors Series, who laundered my typescript and removed several errors and infelicities.

ROBERT L. GALE

University of Pittsburgh

Chronology

1838   John Hay born October 8 in Salem, Indiana, the fourth of six children of Charles Hay (1801 - 1884) and Helen Leonard Hay (1804 - 1893).

1841   Moved with parents to Spunky Point (later called Warsaw), Illinois.

1849   Attended private classical school, Pittsfield, Illinois.

1852   Attended college at Springfield, Illinois, until 1855.

1855   September, entered sophomore class at Brown University.

1858   June, graduated from Brown, as class poet, with master's degree; returned to Warsaw.

1859   Spring, began to read law in Springfield office of uncle, Milton Hay (until early 1861).

1860   Campaigned for Abraham Lincoln after his May nomination as the Republican candidate for president.

1861   February, admitted to Illinois bar; February, appointed by Lincoln to be assistant private secretary and went to Washington, D.C.; March, began to live in White House, until 1865.

1864   January, commissioned major in U.S. Army (promoted to colonel in May, 1865); went on sensitive missions for Lincoln.

1865   Appointed as first secretary of American legation, Paris.

1867   January, left Paris for New York and Washington; June, appointed chargé d'affairs, Vienna.

1868   Traveled in Poland and Turkey; August, resigned and returned to New York and Washington.

1869   June, appointed secretary of American legation, Madrid.

1870   June, left Spain and began editorial work on New York *Tribune*.

1871   October, covered Chicago fire; *Pike County Ballads, Castilian Days*.

1874   February 4, married Clara Louise Stone (1849 - 1914) in Cleveland; made home in New York.

1875   June, moved with Clara to Cleveland.

1879	November, appointed assistant secretary of state by President Rutherford B. Hayes (served until March, 1881); moved to Washington.
1881	April - October, edited New York *Tribune*.
1884	*The Bread-Winners.*
1885	Started hardest work on *Abraham Lincoln: A History*, with John G. Nicolay, until November, 1886.
1886	Moved into fabulous Romanesque house in Washington; *Lincoln* began to appear serially, until 1890.
1890	*Poems; Lincoln* (ten volumes).
1894	Co-edited with Nicolay *Abraham Lincoln: Complete Works* (two volumes).
1897	March, appointed ambassador to England by President William McKinley.
1898	September, became secretary of state under President McKinley and then President Theodore Roosevelt, until July, 1905.
1900	February, signed Hay-Pauncefote Treaty; March, announced acceptance of Open Door Policy; July, dispatched circular on Boxer Rebellion.
1901	April - May, accompanied McKinley on Western campaign tour; November, signed second Hay-Pauncefote Treaty.
1903	January, concluded Hay-Herrán Convention; November, signed Hay-Bunau-Varilla Treaty.
1905	Died July 1 at Lake Sunapee, New Hampshire; buried July 5 in Lake View Cemetery, Cleveland; *Complete Works of Lincoln* (expanded edition, twelve volumes).
1906	*Addresses* (reprinted 1970).
1908	*Letters of John Hay and Extracts from Diary* (three volumes, reprinted 1969).
1910	*A Poet in Exile: Early Letters of John Hay.*
1915	*The Life and Letters of John Hay.*
1916	*The Complete Poetical Works of John Hay* (reprinted 1970).
1938	*A College Friendship: A Series of Letters of John Hay to Hannah Angell.*
1939	*Lincoln and the Civil War in the Diaries and Letters of John Hay* (reprinted 1972).

CHAPTER 1

In Transit, 1838 - 1889

SECRETARY to Lincoln, army colonel, legation officer, short-story writer, poet, travel essayist, journalist and editor, assistant secretary of state, novelist, orator, presidential adviser, biographer and historian, ambassador, secretary of state—John Hay was a man of many talents, interests, opportunities, and accomplishments. In addition, he was so amiable and considerate that he numbered among dozens of personal friends people as diverse as Theodore Roosevelt, William McKinley, Mark Twain, Henry Adams, Henry James, and William Dean Howells.

Hay is not better known today because he scattered his energies. Instead of devoting himself wholly to literature or wholly to diplomacy, he dabbled in poetry, fiction, travel writing, and biography; and, in addition, he was diffident in the realm of public affairs and participated with inexplicable reluctance. As to why Hay behaved as he did, only a partial answer is possible; we need to be aware at the outset, however, that Hay's life conforms to aspects of the American Dream. Hay started humbly in the unwashed Middle West and attained international eminence. He married a millionaire's daughter, had access to enormous wealth, and led their children on paths to status. His attainments may have disquieted him more profoundly than he would admit, but he rationalized his periods of inactivity and self-indulgence on the grounds of sickness. His successes came so effortlessly and he regarded them so lightly that, ultimately, almost nothing he did seemed vital to him—or even an intimate part of himself—and he adopted a disconsolate view of life derived from *Ecclesiastes*. But, in spite of all such attempts at explanation, John Hay still remains a mystery.

I *Boyhood and Education*

John Hay, gentle and poetic by temperament, was born of rugged pioneer stock. His paternal grandfather, also named John, was of

15

"herculean build"; he moved from the Shenandoah Valley to Kentucky, and then to Springfield, Illinois. A farmer, a merchant, an operator of a cotton mill and a brick kiln, he was the father—by his Pennsylvania-bred wife Jemima Coulter Hay—of fourteen children, including one named Charles, born in 1801, who was John Hay's father. His maternal grandfather, David Leonard, was graduated from Brown University; he was a Baptist pastor, a postmaster, and an editor in Massachusetts, New York, and Rhode Island before migrating to Laconia, Indiana, where death severed him from his Massachusetts-bred wife Mary Pierce Leonard and their eleven children, including Helen, Hay's mother.[1]

Hay's father Charles was a student at the classical academy in Lexington, Kentucky; there he mastered Greek and Latin among other subjects before he attended Transylvania University Medical School. In 1829 he migrated to Salem, Indiana, where he became one of three physicians for a population of eight hundred people. A year later, a congenial local lawyer named John Farnham introduced Dr. Hay to his well-educated Eastern wife's unmarried sister Helen Leonard, who had recently moved to Salem and was teaching school there.[2] The two were married in October, 1831. They continued to live in Salem, where their first four children were born; among them was John Milton Hay, who arrived on October 8, 1838. The father added to doctoring the occupations of editing a local paper and of speculating in land; failing in both, he moved with his family in 1841 to Warsaw (then called Spunky Point), Illinois, which was located on the eastern bluffs of the Mississippi River and faced the mouth of the Des Moines River to the west. Little John Hay grew up seeing a variety of migrants, commercial river traffic, black workers, an occasional runaway slave, and tenant farmers under his property-owning father's easy control.[3]

Hay learned a little Latin and Greek and much English literature from his father and from a local schoolmaster. In 1849, his successful lawyer uncle, Milton Hay, invited John to live with him in Pittsfield, Pike County, Illinois, and to attend a good but little private school there. Although his studies at this time did Hay immeasurable good, even more influential were his uncle's stories about such circuit judges and lawyers as Stephen A. Douglas, William Henry Herndon, and Abraham Lincoln; in addition, Hay met John George Nicolay, a local printer's devil. Three years later, Hay moved to Springfield, where he lived with his grandfather and studied at Illinois State University (now Concordia College). A bookish fellow, he wrote stilted, flowery letters home and dreamed of university life in the East. Grandfather Leonard had gone to Brown University, which began as a Baptist institution; so the place seemed ideal—for pedagogical as well as family and religious reasons.[4]

By September, 1855, Hay, not yet seventeen, was penning still more literary epistles home from Providence—this time from 19 University Hall, Brown University, where he had entered the sophomore class, where he had soon become a diligent student, but where he was also sufficiently collegiate to try hashish. He already knew the rudiments of spoken German, in which he had been tutored earlier by an itinerant German teacher. More important, he learned to become a congenial, witty friend, if still an affectedly poetasting one. He met Sarah Whitman, who was then famous for her poetry but who is remembered now only because of her association with Edgar Allan Poe.[5] Hay became class poet; he was graduated in three years with a master's degree; he regarded his education in the East as more important and a better preparation for life than it was. Although he could not realize this fact at the time, the most influential event of his first twenty years was his meeting John Nicolay in Springfield.

Between his departure from Brown and the beginning of the Civil War, Hay loafed at home in Warsaw. He did not wish to teach or preach, and he feared that law might lead to pettifogging. Although he wanted to be an author, he wrote only lugubrious letters to his friends in the East and protested that the barbarous West could not appreciate him. But then, early in 1859, he began reading law with Uncle Milton in Springfield, saw Lincoln in the next-door office of Lincoln-and Herndon, and became friendly with Nicolay, who was then clerking for the Illinois secretary of state and acting as state house librarian.[6]

II   *Four Years with Lincoln*

Hay began his association with Lincoln after the Republican State Convention met at Decatur, Illinois, in May, 1860; backed Lincoln; and thus helped assure his nomination as presidential candidate a little later at the national convention in Chicago. Lincoln was catapulted into national prominence, and so was Springfield. Nicolay was his secretary by this time, and Hay became the secretary's assistant through the campaign. After Lincoln was elected on November 6, he appointed Nicolay his private secretary, and Nicolay persuaded him to let Hay become assistant private secretary. Lincoln is reported to have responded to Nicolay's request thus: "We can't take all Illinois with us down to Washington. Well, let Hay come."[7]

So, one week after passing the Illinois bar on February 4, 1861, the twenty-two-year-old poet *manqué,* having forgotten both his iambs in the excitement of party politics and his dislike of unshorn Westerners in his delight in campaigning before them, was aboard Lincoln's train to Washington and on his way to become a clerk in the Pension Office, Department of the Interior. In January, 1864, he was commissioned major in the United States Army (later lieutenant colonel and, simultaneously, colonel, in May, 1865). When nominally an army officer, he remained on White House assignment as well.[8] In reality, during the war years, Hay was Lincoln's private secretary and personal aide; his courier and intelligence agent; his companion on night walks; his listener, jester, and admirer; and at the last a numb witness at his deathbed. Almost beyond words, Hay came to adore Lincoln for his goodness, patience, understanding, sense of humor, humility, magnanimity, sense of justice, healthy skepticism, resilience and power, love of the common man, and mystical patriotism. In 1866, in a private letter, Hay called Lincoln "the greatest character since Christ."[9]

On several missions for the president, Hay was intelligent and diplomatic. He inspected military and naval facilities in South Carolina and Florida in April and May, 1863; he carried amnesty terms to Floridians willing to swear allegiance in February, 1864; he gathered intelligence on rebel sympathizers among the Order of the American Knights in St. Louis in June, 1864; and he accompanied prickly Horace Greeley, the New York *Tribune* editor and an avowed anti-Lincoln commentator, on an abortive peace mission to the Canadian side of Niagara Falls, in July, 1864.[10] During the war years, it was not all work for Hay; he enjoyed a busy social life, observed the illustrious and the pretentious parading and preening before canny Lincoln, visited Warsaw and Springfield at least three times, and at least twice attended Ford's Theater in Washington with Lincoln—but not on the fatal evening of April 14, 1865.[11]

III   *Europe—To and Fro*

Because Hay had become melancholy and restless well before Appomattox, and because he had desired to avoid irksome red-tape routine and to begin a new chapter, on March 22, 1865, he was happy to accept an appointment to become secretary of legation in Paris. After Lincoln's assassination and his own visit home, Hay arrived in summery Paris to meet his brilliant superior officer, the Minister John Bigelow, whose most delicate task had recently been to counter the persistent efforts of Napoleon III to gain a Mexican toehold in the New World. Hay in his spare time improved his French, sampled French culture, and wrote verse. In December, 1866, when General John A. Dix, Bigelow's replacement, took Hay to meet Napoleon, the young man etched him superbly in his diary.[12]

Hay soon seemed superfluous; so he steamed home, restless yet again. He spent some time early in 1867 in Washington conferring about a new assignment, fretting over militant Germany's rumblings, sizing up Senator Charles Sumner, socializing with respectful President Andrew Johnson, rejecting various commerical offers, and enjoying the attentions of eligible ladies at dances. While home in Warsaw, he read in the New York *Times* that he had been appointed secretary of legation and chargé d'affaires *ad interim* at Vienna.[13]

The Viennese assignment was an educative boondoggle. Hay went to his new station by way of London, where he dined with Charles Francis Adams, the American minister to England and Henry Adams's father; then he traveled to Salisbury, Stonehenge, Antwerp, and Paris, and then to Vienna in August. He was soon improving his off-duty time by polishing his German, strolling through art galleries, attending theater and opera, and touring widely—in Poland, Turkey, and the Alps. His sparkling diary records ingenious, sharp-eyed responses to art, street scenes, soirées, and ecclesiastical and military pomp.[14] Then, as abruptly as fate had handed him the assignment, Hay relinquished it, writing Nicolay in August, 1868: "I have sucked that Austrian orange dry. I don't want to keep wasting good wind on the peel."[15]

Still drifting, Hay returned to America to consider various types of employment—lecturing, another diplomatic post, editorial work. Then, in June, 1869, he was appointed legation secretary at Madrid. Once settled in Madrid a month later, he studied Spanish, watched the unsuccessful struggle of the Republican movement under Emilio Castelar y Ripoll, secretly hoped that Cuban independence might become a reality, and roughed out much of his anticlerical, antimonarchical *Castilian Days*. Although his modest salary curtailed his activities, he enjoyed himself greatly under his immediate

superior General Daniel E. Sickles, a miserable though romantically
wounded Civil War soldier and, of necessity, a passive diplomat in
Spain.[16] In May, 1870, Hay wrote John Bigelow: "I have had a good
year. It is a luxury I can't afford but I can scarcely say I regret it."[17]

After Hay returned to America in September, 1870, his period at
home lasted several years. His literary future began—one for which
his unconscious training had been enviable. Tyler Dennett, Hay's
early biographer, somewhat hastily concludes however, that "In the
intellectual development of the young man these four years [Hay's
forty-eight months in Europe] were more important than the entire
period of his formal education, and perhaps more important also
than service in the White House. When he went to Europe he was
in many ways still a boy; he returned at the age of thirty-two, a
man."[18] Nearly the reverse view might be argued, for Hay had
often served Lincoln with a maturity beyond his years. Thereafter,
he had acted with an instability and with an immaturity that belied
his years, his upbringing, and his experience.

If Hay had been vacillating and unsteady since the end of the
Civil War, he was, from 1871 until shortly after his marriage in
1874, unusually hard-working and purposeful. He began two new
careers—that of popular, controversial man of letters and that of
newspaper editor.

He had always wanted to be a writer, and had published a eulogy
of his friend, the dashing Civil War hero Colonel E. E. Ellsworth, in
the *Atlantic Monthly* in July, 1861,[19] and a good bit of trivial, pleasant verse from that same year forward. Then, late in 1870 and early
the next year he took the country by siege with "Jim Bludso" and
"Little Breeches," poems which became best-selling ones in
pamphlet form. In 1870 and 1871 he also appeared in periodicals
almost twenty times—with installments of *Castilian Days*, poems,
and even a little fiction.[20] In May, 1871, he published *Pike County
Ballads* and, four months later, *Castilian Days*. He also resumed the
lecture circuit, offering "Democracy in Europe," "Franklin in
Paris," and "Phases of Washington Life."[21] Hay's biographer
Dennett concludes that "by the end of 1871 his name was probably
known to as many people in the United States and abroad as in 1897
when he was appointed ambassador to the Court of St. James's."[22]

Moreover, by 1872 Hay had been a respected editor of the New
York *Tribune* for more than a year. There is a charming legend that
Whitelaw Reid, who was virtually the editor of the *Tribune* and
who wanted Hay desperately, had teased him into writing a leader

for an important European dispatch one night; when Greeley, the editor-in-chief and the presiding genius of the paper, read it the next day, he pronounced it the best of the million editorials he had read in a long lifetime. Later Greeley considered Hay to be the most brilliant editor who had ever written for him.[23]

Hay worked well for the *Tribune*, for he met whatever deadlines were imposed on him by his supervisors. Royalties from his two books, combined with his *Tribune* salary of sixty-five dollars a week, enabled him to move from the Astor House to East 25th Street, a better base from which to invade the social and literary circles of New York City. Although his experience in Manhattan disciplined Hay and forced him to compare himself to other necessarily busy men, its greatest gift to him was a series of literary friendships. There, he met Richard Watson Gilder, Clarence King, John La Farge, Augustus St. Gaudens, Bayard Taylor, and Mark Twain, among others. Earlier, in 1861, he had known William Dean Howells, who was soon to be editor of the *Atlantic*, which had published installments of Hay's book about Spain.[24] Only later in Washington did Hay come to know profoundly the man who became his closest friend—Henry Adams.

Two circumstances now intervened to make Hay want to desert writing circles. In the first place, a storm of criticism broke among conservatives because of "Jim Bludso" and "Little Breeches," both of which had appeared in *Pike County Ballads* and both of which were anathematized for alleged vulgarity and subversive theology. In fact, Dennett may not be exaggerating when he concludes that "no author in America was ever more reviled by a conventionally minded public" than Hay was for these poems.[25] Second, Hay had fallen in love, was engaged to be married, and had wearied of the night writing which preceded each morning *Tribune*.

IV   *Marrying Ohio Money*

Hay met Clara Louise Stone (1849 - 1914), the daughter of Amasa and Julia Gleason Stone, at her uncle's New York home, probably in the winter of 1871 - 1872. Shortly before their marriage, in Cleveland on February 4, 1874, he wrote to Reid about her with characteristic wit and self-revelation: "The fact of being in love, and seeing a good woman in love also, is a wonderfully awakening thing. I would not have died before this happened for a great deal of coin." To Nicolay, he wrote that "she is a very estimable young

person—large, handsome, and good. I never found life worth while
before." The couple began married life in New York, and Hay
nominally continued his relationship with the *Tribune* for a while.
But, by the spring of 1875, he was again passively letting fate tell
him what to do: he and his wife moved to Cleveland on a long-term
basis; and he became a business associate of his aggressive, abrasive,
self-made millionaire father-in-law Amasa Stone. Hay described his
new vocation accurately when he wrote Reid that he was "now
ready to skin the pensive Buckeye with neatness and dispatch."
Back in 1858, he had written a Providence friend that "in a few
years [I] will find my eye not rolling in a fine [poetic] frenzy, but
steadily fixed on the pole-star of humanity,$!" Much later, Hay
flattered Ohioans at an Ohio Society Banquet in New York by calling their state "the right place to be married in."[26]

Hay seemed like a heaven-sent replacement to Amasa Stone for
his son Adelbert, who had drowned while at Yale University in
1865. The son-in-law, chameleon enough to get along well with
Stone, allowed him to build the Hays a fabulous mansion on
fashionable Euclid Avenue in Cleveland, in 1876. Hay acted as
Stone's talented public-relations man, and the two men also at-
tempted—without much success—to socialize. Hay sought out the
best minds and wittiest conversationalists that Cleveland could
muster, joined its Vampire Club, and also began dilatorily to
collaborate with Nicolay on their life of Lincoln.[27]

The Hays enjoyed a most happy marriage, and there were even-
tually four children: Helen Hay Whitney (1875 - 1944), Adelbert
Stone Hay (1876 - 1901), Alice Hay Wadsworth Boyd (1880 - 1960),
and Clarence Leonard Hay (1883 - 1969). Clara, according to
Dennett,

. . . was, above all else, "good" in her eager desire to serve John Hay's
welfare. In thirty years she seems never to have interposed a personal
preference which could thwart his well-being. . . . Her part was to follow
her husband, make a perfect home, manage a household as her father had
managed railroads, keep the shutters from banging, buy the railway tickets,
rear quietly the children whom he loved pathetically but never disciplined,
take him to the church which he never joined, and protect him from excur-
sions which would have dissipated his strength and, quite likely, would
have ruined him. . . . Mrs. Hay was not what is called an intellectual
woman and did not share in his literary work, but without her, it is unlikely
that he would have finished his part of *Abraham Lincoln: A History*. She
was not a woman to put her husband forward, and shared in his political
life only as it became necessary to do her part, but, without her, it is almost

inconceivable that John Hay ever would have been Secretary of State for almost seven years.[28]

Meanwhile, Hay dabbled in Ohio politics, which in the late 1870s was an uneasy sea of strange fish. Like other *Tribune* men, Hay had opposed Ulysses S. Grant and therefore the Republican party center. So, when Greeley ran against Grant in 1872, Hay gave him overt support and the loan of his ready pen. But two days after Grant won the election, Greeley died; the infighting for control of the newspaper that followed cost Hay some of his high-flown principles and revered independence—though his friend Reid won the editorship and though the paper nominally became "independent Republican." Then Ohio claimed Hay for a while—an Ohio that, as Dennett points out, "was . . . by far the best State for a man to take up residence in, if he had in mind a political career. It is now by no means a rash guess that John Hay might have been a President of the United States if in 1875 he had seen his opportunity and had been willing to pay the price."[29] But Hay was neither pragmatic nor steadily energetic. He also lacked interest. Furthermore, by 1875 he was also rich and indolent.

Hay oddly supported James G. Blaine instead of Rutherford B. Hayes of Ohio in the 1876 Republican party presidential primaries, but he voted for Hayes—not for the Democratic candidate Samuel J. Tilden—and was happy to see yet another personal acquaintance of his in the White House. But President Hayes did not become instantly friendly in return; Hay had to campaign for the party in various Ohio locales in order to try for what he now restlessly craved—"a second-class [foreign diplomatic] mission," as he wrote Reid in 1879.[30] Instead, a different kind of success rewarded his eloquence when the position of assistant secretary of state in Secretary William H. Evarts's office suddenly became empty. Hayes and Evarts were willing to accommodate faithful Hay, and in November, 1879, the opening was his. He moved with Clara to Washington, D.C.; and served indifferently until another Ohioan, James A. Garfield, became president a year and a half later.

V *More Vacillating*

Hay chafed under Evarts, declined to run for Congress from Ohio in 1880, and refused to become President Garfield's private secretary. In letters to the president-elect, Hay pleaded unfitness for public office, stated his dislike of congressmen, and told about his sickness. Shortly after Garfield's inauguration, Hay moved from Washington[31] to New York to become the temporary editor of the *Tribune* while his friend Reid honeymooned in Europe for six months. Hay helped to steady Garfield's rocky administration by skillful editorializing.[32] A month after Garfield was assassinated, Hay returned the *Tribune* to Reid and made plans to take his family to England and France.

Once abroad, Hay relaxed and evidently wrote in some haste *The Bread-Winners*. He had already published five effective short stories, but he should have produced more in that genre. Thomas Bailey Aldrich, editor of the *Atlantic* by this time, wanted Hay's novel, since Howells had recommended the anonymous work; but Aldrich asked as a prerequisite that the author reveal his name. Squeamish Hay refused, and Richard Watson Gilder, editor of the *Century Magazine*, grabbed the windfall and published *The Bread-Winners* serially from August, 1883, through January, 1884. The novel was then issued in book form, still without Hay's name, by Harper's, officially in January, 1884, but probably in time for the Christmas season, though surely without much expectation that ordinary people would relish its antilabor sentiments.[33] Meanwhile, the Hays had returned home in May, 1883, to be greeted in New York with the hideous news that Clara's father Amasa Stone had committed suicide. At his death, he left $6 million to be divided by Clara Hay and her sister Flora Stone Mather, plus a $500,000 bequest to Hay personally.[34]

The Bread-Winners became immensely popular because of the current labor unrest that it dramatized, because of its sparkling style, and because of its mysterious anonymity. Although Hay might have capitalized upon the success of the novel by publicly acknowledging that he had written it, this possible use may be the reason he only tardily and unofficially revealed his authorship. An editor, writing just after the death of President William McKinley's Vice President Garrett A. Hobart, extolled Hay, who as secretary of state had thus become first in presidential succession, and added: " 'The Bread-Winners,' a striking [sic] story of Cleveland life, whose authorship was long a literary mystery, Colonel Hay has also [with certain fugitive poetry] acknowledged."[35] As the son-in-law of a vicious robber baron, Hay may have lacked the nerve to admit responsibility for fictively demeaning his country's "have-nots." At any rate, he turned to a more important literary venture—his monumental collaboration with John Nicolay on their life of Lincoln.

VI   *Lincoln Work*

Nicolay, the marshal of the United States Supreme Court since 1872, had assiduously collected materials about Lincoln and had consulted nearby archives for some years. Hay, as the more affluent of the two, had been collecting rare materials, both unpublished and published, for about a decade. But delays continued to intervene. In the summer of 1876, when Hay tried to write a few pages, partial blindness drove him from work until fall. A year later he wrote Nicolay that he had resumed but had composed only a few thousand words. In 1879, he again wrote his partner: "I wish I could see you for a week in regard to two or three matters—but I dread journeys more than I can tell you. I get along well enough from day to day, but a change upsets me and gives me colds and insomnia. Where does your work begin—that is, where is my work to join yours, *quoad* Lincoln? How far am I to write his biography before reaching your history of the g-r-r-eat conflict?"[36] Then, a few months later, when Hay went to Washington to work in the Department of State, *Abraham Lincoln: A History* came to a virtual standstill. Next came his editorial stint at the *Tribune,* nearly a year in Europe, and *The Bread-Winners.*

In January, 1884, Hay wrote a letter to Lincoln's son Robert T. Lincoln inviting him to edit the biographical chapters concerning his father:

N[icolay] tells me he has laid before you or is about to do so, the first volumes of our history containing the chapters in which I have described the first forty years of your father's life. I need not tell you that every line has been written in a spirit of reverence and regard. Still you may find here and there words or sentences which do not suit you. I write now to request that you will read with a pencil in your hand and strike out everything to which you object. I will adopt your view in all cases whether I agree with it or not, but I cannot help hoping you will find nothing objectionable.[37]

Here, almost at the outset, Hay reveals his intention to produce a smooth, acceptable family portrait of Lincoln, whose old law partner William Herndon later commented, when the Nicolay-Hay book began to appear serially, "They are aiming, first, to do a superb piece of literary work; second, to make the story with the classes as against the masses. It will result in delineating the real Lincoln about as well as does a wax figure in a museum. . . . Nicolay and Hay handle things with silken gloves and a camel-hair pencil. They do not write with an iron pen. . . . They are writing the Life of Lincoln under the surveillance of Bob Lincoln. He gives them materials and they in turn play hush."[38]

By the spring of 1885, Gilder of the *Century* was dickering with Hay and Nicolay for serial rights; in addition, Harper and Brothers were after book rights—which they failed to obtain. Meanwhile, one of the biggest literary problems that the two writers had to wrestle with involved thoroughness of detail and artistic balance. Nicolay would evidently not have minded making the work three million words in length; Hay constantly favored condensation for proportion, even deletion—to be done with it. Month after month they exchanged chapters, disagreed, and compromised amicably. As an early commentator remarks, "The preface to the ten volumes is a frank declaration of their joint work. There are separate sections written by each, but no key to the distribution except such internal evidence as a shrewd critic may discover."[39]

In November, 1885, Hay and Nicolay signed with the *Century,* which agreed to serialize a generous fraction of the projected total book, to do so over a four-year period, and to pay $50,000 in royalties. Soon after the first installment appeared in November, 1886, Hay began to sicken of the whole procedure; he finally gave Gilder and his staff permission to "whack" as they pleased but not to make him rewrite anything.[40] Page-proofing of the volumes tortured the impatient and uneasy man late into 1889. He wrote Henry Adams in August: "There is nothing left but to read proof and get it printed, which will take six months,—and forgotten, which may take six weeks." But then he wrote Robert Lincoln in December: "They are putting the book into type as fast as we can revise and read the proof, but it is an enormous job, and will require several months to complete it. Think of reading, carefully and critically. . . , five thousand pages, four times over! This we have to do, *after* the book is finished."[41] The Century Company finally published the ten-volume monster, a couple of volumes at a time, late in 1890. A company brochure advertised the set, at thirty dollars, as containing ninety-five wholly or partly new chapters, or roughly forty percent of the total.[42]

The enervating work paid Hay well in cash and in prestige. He received his share of the serial rights and royalties on a rapid subscription sale of over five thousand sets. As biography, it was the longest ever written up to that time in America; as history, it was longer than anything William Hickling Prescott had written, and it vied in length with Francis Parkman's multivolumed narrative of the French and Indian War. Hay was showered with compliments, though such a piecemeal work of joint authorship also evoked some detractions. Of more joy to Hay than income or accolades was the resulting political praise. As Dennett indicates, "He became [through his *Lincoln*] the apostle of the Republican party, so to be regarded to the end of his days."[43]

CHAPTER 2

In State, 1890 - 1905

ALTHOUGH it is tempting to theorize that ennui caused Hay to suffer sustained melancholy after the completion of *Lincoln,* he actually was plagued by weltschmerz and by a half-whimsical schizophrenia most of his life.[1] He seemed to grow worse until the spring of 1897, when McKinley appointed him ambassador to England.

I *Dilettantism*

Hay had for a long interval been harmlessly occupied. He spoiled his four sturdy children; traveled extensively; summered at the Fells, his rambling Newbury, New Hampshire, vacation home near Lake Sunapee; went hunting every fall; studied national and international politics; and happily socialized in Washington. Three of the closest friends of John and Clara Hay were Clarence King and Henry and Marian Adams. Together they formed the so-called Five of Hearts, a secret little association, which once inspired Adams to write pleasantly to Hay that "the universe hitherto has existed in order to produce a dozen people to amuse the five of hearts. Among us, we know all mankind. We or our friends have canvassed creation, and there are but a dozen or two companions in it. . . ."[2]

Hay was always a considerate friend. Clarence King, geologist, mining engineer, traveler, and idolized friend of the tolerant great, died in 1901. While he was gravely ill in California, he wrote Hay a rambling letter which goes in part thus: "Of your generosity and kindness to me I am always thinking, and always grateful. It seems superhuman to me and perhaps it is." When Mrs. Adams committed suicide in 1885, Hay wrote her stunned husband as follows: "I hoped all day yesterday and this morning to hear from you, and thought it possible you might summon K[ing] and me to be with you at the last. . . . I can neither talk to you nor keep silent. The darkness in which you walk has its shadow for me also. You and your wife were more to me than any other two. I came to Washington [in 1879] because you were there. . . ."³ Marian Adams never lived in the famous home designed for the Adamses by Henry Hobson Richardson next door to its twin simultaneously built for the Hays in Washington. The mansions were not ready for occupancy until 1886, but they immediately became architectural wonders, the source of much public curiosity, and the official Washington residences of Adams (1603 H Street) and the Hays (800 Sixteenth Street). On Lafayette Square, their mansions were within view of the White House.

For a full decade before his appointment in 1897 as ambassador to England, Hay was lazy and uncertain. He made it a hobby to back unsuccessful political candidates by preferring Blaine to Garfield in 1880, Blaine to Grover Cleveland in 1884, John Sherman to Benjamin Harrison in 1888, and Harrison (with Hay's old friend Reid as vice-presidential running mate) to Cleveland in 1892. So it was not until McKinley, an Ohio friend of years' standing, became president that Hay was again in a position to expect a reward for party loyalty. Vacationing in England in the summer of 1896, he found time to write to the London *Times;* and it printed on June 1 his prediction that McKinley would be nominated and would then win the presidency. Hay added, "We who know him regard him as a man of extraordinary ability, integrity and force of character, and have no hesitation in predicting for him an administration in a high degree wise, pure, politic and magnanimous." A few weeks before William Jennings Bryan of "Cross of Gold" fame was defeated, Hay, back home again, wrote more privately to Adams from Cleveland: "I spent yesterday with the Majah [McKinley had been a Civil War brevet major]. . . . I was more struck than ever with his mask. It is a genuine Italian ecclesiastical face of the fifteenth century. . . . You are not interested in political news. If you were, I would give you a political pointer. The Majah has a cinch—and don't you forget it."⁴

All this analysis suggests such familiarity with McKinley that it should have surprised no one when the victor appointed Hay to the Court of St. James's in March, 1897.

II   *Mr. Ambassador*

Dennett regards Hay's seventeen months as ambassador as "the happiest . . . of his life. At last he had found gaiety, mixed with

enough of serious purpose to satisfy all sides of his nature. His
health, while by no means perfect, was greatly improved. The note
of frustration and despair disappeared from his letters. All his varied
experiences of more than half a century had combined to prepare
him for the rôle to which he had been assigned, and he carried it
easily."[5]

While ambassador, Hay performed official duties, lolled about in
sociable idleness, and traveled. Being literary, he was welcomed by
British leaders of government and society as perhaps the most popular American ambassador since James Russell Lowell. Queen Victoria is said to have called Hay "the most interesting of all the Ambassadors I have known."[6] His conversation sparkled with tactful
wit. He spoke engagingly in May at the unveiling of Sir Walter
Scott's bust in Westminster Abbey. The following winter, he took
an extended tour with his wife and the Adamses up the Nile River;
he was relaxing in faraway Egypt when the news reached him that
the *Maine* had sunk in Havana harbor. He leisurely returned to his
London desk in mid-March, while the Adamses drifted on to Beirut,
Damascus, and Greece.[7]

Queen Victoria contributed indirectly to Hay's becoming
McKinley's new secretary of state. When Hay's friend Reid wanted
to wangle himself a position as the special envoy to her Diamond
Jubilee, Hay, though privately scornful of the pomposity of the
celebration, did much more than he needed to promote the vain
man's cause. McKinley was so touched that when he wrote two long
personal letters to Hay he observed in the second that his ambassador's conduct "will in the end I am sure strengthen your own
position." Less than three weeks later, the president cabled Hay an
offer to make him secretary of state.[8]

Believe it or not, Hay penned a note to McKinley pleading poor
health and declining an offer that must have struck him as the
culmination of a career of president-watching and of studying international affairs. But, after he had thought about the invitation and
had perhaps conferred with friends, Hay dispatched a gracious
acceptance. About both of Hay's messages, Dennett has observed
that "the two draft telegrams present in the most graphic way the
great underlying conflict which had embroiled Hay's life for forty
years: on the one hand, love of ease; on the other, sense of
duty. . . . Somewhere in him was a hero. . . . Now, at the age of
sixty, his . . . chance had come. He faltered, but only for a
moment."[9]

III   *Mr. Secretary*

Hay called the Spanish-American War "a splendid little war." Out of context, this famous phrase sounds callous; but in actuality, he wrote Teddy Roosevelt in July, 1898, as follows: "It has been a splendid little war; begun with the highest motives, carried on with magnificent intelligence and spirit, favored by that Fortune which loves the brave. It is now concluded, I hope, with that fine good nature, which is, after all, the distinguishing trait of the American character." During most of the conflict, Hay had been on the sidelines watching international intrigues that primarily involved others. In May, he had written from London to a friend, "I detest war, and had hoped I might never see another, but this was as necessary as it was righteous. I have not for two years seen any other issue." [10]

By the time Hay was sworn in as secretary of state on September 30, the dissolution of the Spanish Empire in the Caribbean and the Philippines had been accomplished, and the machinery was set in motion which resulted in the Treaty of Peace that was signed in Paris in December, 1898. The war had been popular in the United States. Victory skyrocketed the renown of Hay's friend, McKinley, but its results permanently altered the current of American affairs in the family of nations. Spain granted Cuba its independence and ceded Puerto Rico, Guam, and the Philippines to the United States for $20 million; and, when America developed into a power in the Pacific, the commercial, naval, military, and political consequences became what Hay called a "cosmic tendency." [11] When he became a cabinet member under a popular president, he inherited diplomatic difficulties unmatched since the Civil War.

President Theodore Roosevelt retained Hay as secretary of state, although the strenuous executive had mixed feelings about his refined subordinate. Roosevelt wrote Hay on two separate occasions in 1899 and 1900: "You have indeed led a life eminently worth living, oh, writer of books and doer of deeds!—and, in passing, builder of beautiful houses and father of strong sons and fair daughters." "You have been the greatest Secretary of State I have seen in my time. . . ." Yet, rather soon after Hay's death, Roosevelt pontificated in a letter to Henry Cabot Lodge that Hay "was not a great Secretary of State. . . . He had a very ease-loving nature and a moral timidity which made him shrink from all that was rough in life, and therefore from practical affairs. . . . [H]is temptation was to associate as far as possible only with men of refined and cultivated tastes, who lived apart from the world of affairs, and who, if Americans, were wholly lacking in robustness of fibre.''[12]

All the same, Hay knew American diplomatic history and was therefore aware of the country's long-standing problems. During his seven-year tenure, he tackled most of them, as we shall see, and he also had to face several new ones. The trouble spots of the greatest significance included Colombia, the Philippines, and China. The following generally chronological narrative shows the official role he played from October, 1898, until his death in July, 1905, as secretary of state under President McKinley and then under President Roosevelt. As will be seen, Hay was in favor of American imperialism, was pro-English, and was apprehensive about Germany and Russia.[13] Moreover, he was periodically melancholy, intermittently anxious to get out of office, and pathetically sick.

IV   1898 - 1900

On October 1, 1898, when Hay assumed his duties as secretary of state, he must have uneasily thought about McKinley's remark that state matters were no longer a worry now that Hay was on hand. But Hay knew that he could rely on Alvey A. Adee, long a close friend and second assistant secretary of state, and on Henry White, then first secretary of the American Embassy in London and another old friend.[14] Nonetheless, Hay quickly established a grueling regimen, for he was plagued by office-seekers, favor-askers, and log-rolling senators. By November, he had learned about the worsening Chinese situation through pro-American Lord Charles Beresford, who was traveling in the Far East and who reported that the other major powers in the area might soon start to partition China.

A month later, Hay requested White to sound out Lord Salisbury, then prime minister of England, about his country's willingness to abrogate the Clayton-Bulwer Treaty, which guaranteed that any canal built to join the Atlantic and the Pacific Oceans would be jointly controlled but open to all nations. Hay was overjoyed to learn that both Salisbury and Sir Julian Pauncefote, British ambassador to the United States, were favorably disposed to such an abrogation. Meanwhile, Hay had been learning of German ambitions in the Philippines, and he began to reactivate negotiations to modify the untenable condominium by which the United States,

England, and Germany controlled the Samoan Island harbor facilities.[15]

There was no let-up for Hay of problems in 1899. In January, Hay fenced by letter with ambitious Reid while he had Joseph H. Choate, a better man for the job, appointed ambassador to England. Hay also had to curry favor with Senator John T. Morgan, who had long been maneuvering to advance his lifelong project of a Nicaraguan canal rather than a Panamanian one. February saw the permanent adjournment of the commission that had been meeting in Quebec and then Washington to discuss Alaskan boundary disagreements among Canada, England, and the United States. In July, Alfred E. Hippisley, another Britisher familiar with Chinese affairs, conferred with Hay about a policy toward that troubled empire. Within weeks—on September 6, to be exact—Hay issued the famous circular letter verbalizing the Open Door Policy, which permitted all nations to trade in China and which assured his fame.[16]

About a month later, the miserable war erupted between England and the Boers in South Africa. Liberal Democrats in America found in the occasion an opportunity to criticize Hay, who had hoped, just before hostilities, that, "if it comes to blows, . . . England will make quick work of Uncle Paul [Kruger, President of Transvaal]." After the war had started, Hay complained to Choate that, when England suffered a couple of minor setbacks, "the welkin rings with outcry against her, flavored with a brogue, and the lower breed of politicians begin to join the outcry. A smashing victory would quiet everything considerably. . . ."[17] Whether Hay realized it or not, the entanglement of England in South Africa restrained Queen Victoria's hand elsewhere, all of which helped America emerge as a world power around 1900. In November, 1899, Hay opened inconclusive negotiations to buy the Danish Islands; but, during this time, he was able to congratulate himself for his easy part in the partition of the Samoan Islands. By terms of the treaty, the United States obtained Tutuila, which included the magnificent harbor of Pago Pago.[18]

In January, 1900, Hay queried Choate about British sentiments concerning the Hay-Pauncefote Treaty, which gave their two countries the exclusive right to build a canal across Central America to connect the Atlantic and the Pacific; he seemed happy that the American reply to Salisbury had nullified illicit Canadian ambitions to arbitrate the Alaskan boundary quarrel; and he privately worried about Russian hypocrisy toward the Open Door Policy. On

February 5, he and Pauncefote signed their first canal treaty, which was then attacked and amended by the U.S. Senate, and finally rejected by England. In March, Hay cleverly offered to act as arbitrator in the Boer War; he was courteously told by Salisbury to stay out, and thereafter could—and often did—asseverate that America had tried for peace and had thereafter to keep hands off.[19] He was so upset when the first Hay-Pauncefote Treaty was doomed that he offered McKinley his formal resignation, which the president declined, saying, "Nothing could be more unfortunate than to have you retire from the Cabinet. . . . Your record constitutes one of the most important and interesting pages of our diplomatic history."[20]

Although Hay was outraged at newspaper abuse of him in March, he released an Olympian notice that all powers had assented to his Open Door Policy, which he therefore labeled "final and definitive"[21]—with more eloquence than truth. Opinions concerning Hay and the Open Door Policy have been diverse ever since his announcement. Henry Adams wrote that "the agreement binds no one to anything, and perhaps that is the reason why everybody assents." And an authority on Brooks Adams, Henry's brother, believes that "Hay must have realized the essential emptiness of his policy, for he could hardly miss understanding that not he but European politics had produced what little deference was given the Open Door."[22] But a Far Eastern expert says that, when the Russians failed to evacuate Manchuria in 1903, they "broke their [Open Door] promise." And yet a distinguished diplomatic historian actually defines the Open Door Policy as "a pious hope rather than a stern international reality." George Kennan was perhaps closest to reality when he criticized the adverse effects of the policy on American diplomacy but placed much of the blame on the callowness of the American public for accepting the policy as a supposed Yankee coup. He also thought that it created a dangerous myth, that Hay quickly became disillusioned, and that the American government not only failed to implement the Open Door Policy but in fact subsequently departed from it.[23]

Hay soon had to face his most dramatic diplomatic challenge—the consequences of the Chinese Boxer Rebellion, an uprising against foreigners in 1900. Dennett efficiently notes that between the attack on the foreign legations in Peking and their rescue, "Hay made four moves on the international chessboard, each one favored by the usual Hay luck, which, together, built up his policy."[24] First, he ordered on June 10 that the American minister in the Chinese capital engage in no alliances, but protect American lives and interests. Second, on July 3, he countered foreign efforts to divide China with his declaration that "Chinese territorial and administrative entity" had to be preserved and that "equal and impartial trade in all parts of the Chinese Empire" had to be safeguarded.[25] Third, because he declined to believe that the Boxers had massacred all the foreigners in Peking, he sent the American minister there a request for information through a cleverly circuitous route. Nine days later, on July 20, Hay rejoiced when he received his reply through the Chinese legation in Washington: the foreigners were alive, though in dire need of relief. And fourth, Hay, on August 4, urged McKinley to reopen communication lines and to cooperate with the international relief forces that were starting to move from Tientsin.[26]

Thus, more than any other man alive, Hay maintained the uneasy Far Eastern status quo. Adams wrote him from Paris in late June: "You've got literally the world on your shoulders." But the effort almost cost Hay his life. In addition to exhaustion he was suffering from prostatism; it was not until October that he could resume his official duties.[27]

In November, Hay again tried—without success—to buy the elusive Danish Islands. In December, when Paul Kruger, president of the Transvaal and hence England's Boer War opponent, signaled his desire to visit America, Anglophile Hay tried to block the move privately, and McKinley intervened to support him. At about this time, Hay continued to think dyspeptically about senatorial efforts to amend the beauty and gentlemanliness of his canal treaty with Pauncefote. Hay was especially upset because he had also just signed delicate collateral protocols with Nicaragua and Costa Rica, which would have been advantageous to the United States if the treaty had ever become law, and if the canal had thereafter been built along Hay-Pauncefote specifications.[28]

V   *1901 - 1903*

The year 1901 was marked by tragedy for Hay. In March, he was dismayed at McKinley's decision to withdraw all American troops from China except a small legation guard. In April, after England had rejected the canal treaty, Hay sat down with Pauncefote to draft a revision that was signed and ratified by both signatories later in the year; but this time Hay had wisely conferred with Lodge and others, who properly insisted on fortification rights. Hay, in May, sent Pauncefote a new Alaskan treaty; and he was soon pleased to learn that England was becoming amenable to reason about territory north of Puget Sound. During the same month, Hay communicated with Peking on the subject of Chinese indemnities following the Boxer Rebellion.[29]

Then came June 23, 1901, the saddest day in Hay's life. His older son Adelbert "Del" Hay had graduated from Yale University three years before, was subsequently his father's secretary in London, and then became American consul at Pretoria, South Africa. When Del returned to the United States in 1900, McKinley named him his assistant secretary. While Del was attending an alumni reunion at Yale, he evidently sat on a hotel windowsill to enjoy cool air before retiring that fatal evening; he dozed or otherwise slipped, and fell to his death.[30] Hay never recovered from this blow, nor did his wife Clara, to whom Adams wrote piercingly: "Of course, all turns on you. If you break down, John will break down."[31]

Life and death went on. McKinley was shot in Buffalo, New York, lingered a few days, and died September 14. Hay wrote a British friend, "I wonder how much grief we can endure. It seems to me I am full to the brim. I see no chance of recovery—no return to the days when there seemed something worth while. . . . What a strange and tragic fate it has been of mine—to stand by the bier of three of my dearest friends, Lincoln, Garfield, and McKinley, three of the gentlest of men, all risen to be head of the State, and all done to death by assassins. I think you know Mr. Roosevelt, our new President. He is an old and intimate friend of mine; a young fellow of infinite dash and originality."[32]

Hay would have preferred to resign at once from dashing Teddy's cabinet, but he was bullied into staying in it. Yet, as he wrote Adams, "I can still go at any moment he gets tired of me, or when I collapse."[33] McKinley had been so gentle and conservative that Hay had had to push him into a more imaginative foreign policy. With Roosevelt, the situation was precisely the reverse; and, in addition, Hay by now was a saddened, slowly dying old man.[34]

Hay's first duty to the new president took the form of a tender letter in which he offered congratulations tempered by a tone of sorrow for dead McKinley and his own dead son Del, and ended with a prediction of Rooseveltian glory and his own speedy death.[35] Two months later, in November, Hay signed the second Hay-

Pauncefote Treaty, which was quickly ratified by the Senate. But Hay's dwindling spirits that Christmas were snuffed out entirely by news of the death of his beloved, erratic friend Clarence King.

The years 1902 and 1903 were frenzied ones in the realm of diplomacy. In January, 1901, Hay learned that the New Panama Company was willing to sell its rights; however, he continued to favor the Nicaraguan route. In April, he opened negotiations with the Canal Company to buy construction rights and tactfully wrote pro-Nicaraguan Senator Morgan that Congress must choose the location of any isthmian canal. Hay was delighted when Russia and China signed a pact by virtue of which the Russians promised to leave the Chinese Manchurian territory. Hay sent a representative to Havana in May, thus inaugurating diplomatic relations with Cuba again. In June, Roosevelt sunnily ordered Hay to take charge of Colombian negotiations for canal rights; but the president soon upset him by interfering with the ongoing discussions concerning the Alaskan border. Hay was briefly aghast when he learned in September that American marines were jeopardizing his isthmian maneuverings by landing at Panama to guard a treasured railroad line during the latest revolution in that steamy region. The Colombian ambassador inopportunely chose to be offended and had to be replaced by Tomas Herrán.[36]

Hay suffered two more annoyances in December. He felt obliged to advise Roosevelt to stay out of Venezuela's continuing dispute with Germany and England, and to let the Hague Court handle it. Next, Hay's old adversary, Lodge of Massachusetts, in the name of New England fishermen, blocked Hay's efforts to write a codfish treaty with Newfoundland. These events disillusioned the already acerbic Hay, for he saw in the first incident the danger of a stick-wielding, almost tyrannical president, and in the second affair he found still more proof of the unlikelihood of doing diplomatic business in the presence of partisan legislators.

The new year of 1903 was pivotal for Hay professionally. In February, he met, and immediately liked, the new German ambassador to Washington, Baron Speck von Sternburg. By April, if not earlier, Hay was expressing his fear that America would do nothing about Russian perfidy in northern China. In May, he was on the defensive for his unwillingness to protest the bloody pogrom of Kishinev, in the Russian province of Bessarabia; he rationalized that his hands were tied because Roosevelt was touring in the West, and because Russia might lodge complaints against American mob violence here and there. Hay privately contributed five hundred dollars to a New York Jewish relief committee.[37]

Nothing startling occurred in the late spring. But in July, Hay received this high praise from his unpredictable chief: "When I came in I thought you a great secretary of state, but now I have had a chance to know far more fully what a really great secretary of state you are." Hay's response? Something within him impelled him to suggest Elihu Root as a suitable successor and to offer Roosevelt his resignation, which Teddy wisely refused. "I could not spare you," he replied, perhaps because he knew that Hay had tact and eloquence enough to restrain his chief's thoughtless impetuosity.[38]

New problems reared their hydra heads. In August, the Colombian Senate rejected the Hay-Herrán Treaty, by which Colombia would have ceded to the United States a narrow belt of land across the Panama isthmus. In September, while Hay was at Lake Sunapee, he wrote Roosevelt to restrain him from waving his big stick over Alaska while the border was *sub judice;* less than a month later, the Alaskan tribunal decided in favor of the United States; and Hay was the hero of the week. But in November came the Panamanian revolution, by means of which the Democrats scored points against Roosevelt for his combativeness south of the border, and some of the mud slung at the president hit Hay. All available evidence, however, clears him of complicity in instigating the insurrection. And yet, within sixty hours, Hay signed a telegram authorizing recognition of the new state of Panama—an independent country that quickly agreed to let the United States dig an isthmian canal through its volatile land.[39]

VI *1904 - 1905*

The years 1904 and 1905 were a falling off for Secretary Hay. January found him loyally defending Roosevelt's treatment of Panama. In February, he was watching the Russo-Japanese War with a fixed bias toward Japan, China, England, and France, and against Russia and Germany.[40] During the same month, he was also readying a circular note proposing to exclude Chinese territory from the military theater, and his intent was to keep Russia out of Manchuria. Also that month, the Senate ratified the Hay-Bunau-Varilla Treaty, which granted the United States rights to use, occupy, and control a ten-mile strip of land for a canal. Hay, though sick, had had to dissuade a few greedy senators from wringing more concessions from the Panamanians.[41]

In April, after Roosevelt and certain cabinet members had asked Hay to campaign for the Republican party, the tired diplomat must have relished recording the following in his diary: "It is intolerable that they should not see how much more advantageous to the Administration it is that I should stay at home and do my work than that I should cavort around the country making lean and jejune orations." All the same, Hay betook himself the next month to the World's Fair in St. Louis to present an important address, the point of which was that there is "a cosmic tendency" in men and nations which cannot be withstood—hence America's recently almost illimitable expansionist endeavors.[42]

In June, an international incident occurred upon which Hay capitalized dramatically. When a South Carolinian named Ion H. Perdicaris, who was traveling abroad, was kidnapped by a Moroccan brigand named Raisuli and held for ransom, Hay cabled the American consul in Tangiers: "We want Perdicaris alive or Raisuli dead." Privately calling his action "a concise impropriety," Hay was publicly gratified when Perdicaris was promptly released unharmed. In fact, the man was no longer an American citizen and was not Hay's responsibility. This fact was suppressed for sixteen months, and the entire episode helped Roosevelt to improve his already excellent chances both at the Republican National Convention in Chicago that June and at the polls.[43]

Later in the year and into the next, Baron Kogoro Takahira, the Japanese minister at Washington, asked Hay to urge all powers to let his country maximize its gains because of its military victory over Russia. Hay was happy to comply, but he remained officially neutral.[44]

In 1905, the year of Hay's death, the exhausted diplomat could do little. He barely had strength to attend Roosevelt's inauguration in March, after which he sailed to Europe with his wife in a vain search for health at Bad Nauheim, Germany. He was so weak that he declined invitations to attend official gatherings in Berlin, Paris, Brussels, and London. When he could not call upon King Leopold II of Belgium, the king called upon Hay; Hay later had an interview with the French minister of foreign affairs in Paris and a luncheon with King Edward in Buckingham Palace.[45]

In June, Hay and his devoted wife took passage from Liverpool to America. During the voyage, he dreamed that he reported to his president at the White House, only to notice that it was Lincoln who greeted him—with sympathy as to his health and with some easy letters to answer. Hay, though happy that he could do the work, felt a sense of what he described as "overpowering melancholy." He later reported to Roosevelt, who had written Clara rather muscularly that he would "handle the whole business of the State Department myself this summer."[46] Hay remained in Washington ten days, then crawled by slow train to his beloved Fells in New Hampshire, and caught a cold along the way. Six days later, he proved that the burdens of his important office had indeed been staggering by succumbing to prostate infection, a chronically weakened heart, general poisoning of the system, and finally a blood clot.[47]

Back in 1902, Hay had written his brother-in-law Samuel Mather, "I am getting old. . . . I ought not to grumble. I have reached my grand climacteric with no serious illness, no material bad luck. My dear Del is safe, with a beloved memory and a bright young fame. The girls [his daughters Alice and Helen] are well settled, with excellent men, fellows of heart and conscience. Clarence [his younger son] promises an honorable and tranquil life. I shall not be much missed except by my wife." Then, only a few days before his death on July 1, 1905, Hay wrote in his diary,

I say to myself that I should not rebel at the thought of my life ending at this time. I have lived to be old; something I never expected in my youth. I have had many blessings, domestic happiness being the greatest of all. I have lived my life. I have had success beyond all the dreams of my boyhood. My name is printed in the journals of the world without descriptive qualifications, which may, I suppose, be called fame. By mere length of service I shall occupy a modest place in the history of my time. If I were to live several years more I should probably add nothing to my existing reputation; while I could not reasonably expect any further enjoyment of life, such as falls to the lot of old men in sound health. I know death is the common lot, and what is universal ought not to be deemed a misfortune; and yet—instead of confronting it with dignity and philosophy, I cling instinctively to life and the things of life, as eagerly as if I had not had my chance at happiness and gained nearly all the great prizes.[48]

CHAPTER 3

Literary Friends

JOHN Hay was mourned at his grave in the Lake View Cemetery in Cleveland by President Roosevelt, his vice president, cabinet members, Supreme Court justices, the governor of Ohio, foreign diplomats, family members, and many friends. He was well remembered, for, not quite sixty-seven years of age, he had predeceased most of his friends. They included not merely presidents and kings, ambassadors and military folk, but many writers as well. His four closest literary friends were Henry Adams, Mark Twain, William Dean Howells, and Henry James; but he also knew several others of note.

I Henry Adams

Henry Adams was Hay's closest friend; and, since Adams thought that Hay was "the only man whose society I depend upon," Hay in turn was Adams's closest friend. Born the same year, they first met in Washington early in 1861, and they had much in common. Both had been educated in the East, and both were the secretaries of influential leaders: Hay worked for Lincoln, and Adams had recently begun an eight-year stint as the secretary of his distinguished father, Charles Francis Adams. Both young men were intelligent, witty, passively perceptive observers of history-making events. Both had already begun to write, and soon each began to subject his efforts to the other's irreverent scrutiny.[1]

When Hay and Adams renewed their acquaintance is uncertain—perhaps in London in 1865, but certainly by July, 1867, when both were there. In 1879, perhaps through their mutual friend Clarence King, their casual relationship deepened to such intimacy that the two—with their wives and King—formed the Five of Hearts and became the firmest of friends for a quarter century. They often vacationed together; and, when one was absent from

Washington, they exchanged letters that glow with wisdom, simmer with cynicism, and explode in humor. When Hay became secretary of state, Adams habitually visited him to take tea and offer advice. How much he influenced Hay's foreign policy attitudes is conjectural, but some commentators think that he did so considerably.[2]

When Hay early in 1905 vainly sought health in European spas, Adams accompanied him; and Clara Hay, Adams wrote to a friend, "appealed to me for help, and I could not refuse. Between us, or rather by her energy, we overrode law and state, so that we dragged Hay to sea." When the two friends had to be separated because Adams was bound for Paris, Hay wrote their mutual friend, the sculptor Augustus Saint-Gaudens, "My doctor . . . says there is nothing the matter with me except old age, the Senate, and two or three other mortal maladies, and so I am going to N[auheim] to be cured of all of them. This involves parting with the Porcupinus Angelicus [Adams]—and I would almost rather keep the diseases. He has been kindness itself. . . ." Adams agreed that Hay might have lived longer had he not confined himself to an office in which he was badgered by Roosevelt and many senators; but, as Adams later noted, Hay "kept himself there [in the State Department] . . . because he was afraid of being bored."[3]

When Hay had died, word quickly reached Adams in Paris, and he wrote to Clara Hay that, "As for me, it is time for me to say goodbye. I am tired. My last hold on life is lost with him. . . . He and I began life together. We will stop together." Adams's more public statements about his most intimate friend are contained in the seven symphonic paragraphs that close his *Education of Henry Adams*. In them he reviews their last season together; comments on his friend's fame and power; and, after asserting that his own education has ended, lapses into "Hamlet's Shakespearean silence."[4]

The final lines of the *Education* make no mention, however, of Hay's literary accomplishments. Elsewhere, Adams noted a few praiseworthy items in his friend's writings, as when he singled out three poems—"Jim Bludso," "Little Breeches," and the later "Israel"—for specific comment. When speculation was running wild as to the authorship of Adams's anonymously published novel *Democracy* in 1880, Adams giggled with delight that Hay was named as a possibility; but Adams barely mentioned *Castilian Days*—and then only in passing.[5]

The Adamses, particularly Henry, and the Hays enjoyed an incredible joke that arose from the anonymity of the author of *The Bread-Winners*. Adams's brother Charles Francis Adams, Jr., not privy to the secrets of the Five of Hearts, wrote a letter to the editor of the *Nation*, on February 21, 1884, in which he harshly criticized the author of *The Bread-Winners* and accused him of having also written *Democracy*.[6] Hay may have undertaken to write *The Bread-Winners* because Adams had written *Democracy*, and he may have published it anonymously to supply more fun for the Five of Hearts. Pretending that Hay had written *Democracy*, Adams wittily warned him: "Is it not a little risky for your anonymity to lay the scene [of *The Bread-Winners*] at Cleveland after laying the scene of *Democracy* at Washington?" Adams criticized minor weaknesses in *The Bread-Winners* while cursorily praising its "composition, style, and general handling."

Specific praise for Hay as the anonymous author of *Bread-Winners* appears in only one letter from Adams to Hay, and those good words were delivered at the expense of Howells and James. Lauding Hay's "skill in construction, vivacity in narration, and breadth of *motif*," Adams ruthlessly added that "It has also one curious and surprising quality, least to be expected from an unknown western writer. Howells cannot deal with gentlemen or ladies; he always slips up. James knows almost nothing of women but the mere outside; he never had a wife. This new writer not only knows women, but knows *ladies*; the rarest of literary gifts. I suppose he has an eastern wife?" Finally, still maintaining the fiction of authorial mystery, Adams discarded the possibility that *The Bread-Winners* had been written by a woman because he thought the author displayed a "sense of humor . . . markedly masculine."[7]

As for *Abraham Lincoln: A History* by Nicolay and Hay, Adams regarded this work as the capstone of his friend's literary labors. From humid Washington in July, 1890, he wrote to a friend that "Hay also remains here, held by the last sheets of his great work." In 1892, when Adams declined an honorary degree from Harvard University, a proffered reward for his own historical researches, which had culminated in *History of the United States during the Administrations of Jefferson and Madison* (nine volumes, 1889 - 1891), he suggested that Hay was more deserving. Two years later Adams refused a Columbia University honorary degree and again offered Hay's name instead. At least twice more, Adams linked himself and Hay as fellow historians. He wrote his brother Brooks Adams, "I never yet heard of ten men who had ever read my history and never one who had read Hay's *Lincoln.*" And he boasted in his *Education* that in 1892,

Hay himself was almost as languid and indifferent as Adams. Neither had occupation. Both had finished their literary work. The "Life" of Lincoln had been begun, completed, and published hand in hand with the "History" of Jefferson and Madison, so that between them they had written nearly all the American history there was to write. The intermediate period needed intermediate treatment; the gap between James Madison and Abraham Lincoln could not be judicially filled by either of them. Both were heartily tired of the subject, and America seemed as tired as they.[8]

Shortly after Hay's death, his widow persuaded Adams to edit her husband's letters. She loaned him bundles of retrieved epistles, and he lavished much leisure in Washington and Paris transcribing scores of them. The deed had its rewards; for, as an Adams biographer observes, "Working with this material, Adams felt his dead friend's attitudes come alive again in his hands. He experienced again Hay's gift for nonsense and also his gift for somberness."[9] But Adams also had his fears; for, as he wrote Whitelaw Reid and Henry White, the recipients of some of Hay's confidential missives, friends and even government officials "might find certain epithets keen," and Clara Hay might see fit to censor the letters rather freely.[10] And she did! She deleted "goddams," "hells," a comment about "sparking" in rural Illinois, and certain diplomatic indiscretions. She also substituted initials for the names of still living persons in order to protect them, and rather amusingly, avoided naming all real places and even journals. Thus, we read, for example, "This morning I read in the little *H*——— that W——— M——— has been made Ambassador at R———. . . ."[11]

Edmund Wilson was not often wrong, but he was a hundred percent in error when he accepted Herbert Croly's anecdote. Croly, after interviewing Adams, claimed he got the impression that Adams regarded Hay as "a mediocre person."[12] Quite the contrary view is obtained by reading the masses of Adams material, for the readers find in it the flow of unmistakable friendship and admiration. Hay and Adams disagreed on occasion, but the following two statements from Adams to Hay have the ring of complete sincerity: "St. Thomas Aquinas and you are my only friends," and, "In short, my venerable friend I respect and admire you beyond measure. . . ."[13]

II   *Mark Twain*

A proof of Hay's tolerance was his ability to be both Adams's closest friend and one of Mark Twain's admired acquaintances. Hay and Twain had profoundly similar environments: both were products of the Middle West, and they actually spent their early years only a short distance apart. As Twain once wrote to their mutual friend William Dean Howells, "I was born & reared at Hannibal, & John Hay at Warsaw, 40 miles higher up, on the [Mississippi] river (one of the Keokuk [Iowa] packet ports). . . ." Amusingly, Twain was wrong about Hay's birthplace, which was really Salem, Indiana, and also his own—Florida, Missouri. Shortly before Hay's death, Twain sent him a touching, unsigned letter in which he complimented Hay for being universally esteemed, for having unquestionable motives, and for deserving a nation's gratitude.[14]

When the two men first met is uncertain. One biographer writes that "Hay and Twain met in 1867 and were close friends by the 1870s," but offers no proof. After Hay's death in 1905, Twain released a statement to the press that, "My friendship with Mr. Hay & my admiration of him endured 38 years without impairment."[15] At any rate, they were surely friends by 1871. The previous summer, Twain amiably criticized Hay for making Jim Bludso an engineer instead of a pilot, and the poet defended his choice in a reply to "Mr. Clemens" that is dated January 8, 1871, and is from the *Tribune* office. Hay also wrote enigmatically about " 'ribaldry' 'plagiarism B.H [Bret Harte]' and 'vulgar blasphemy' "; but whether Bret Harte was accusing Hay or Twain, or was answering some accusation, is unclear.[16] In March, 1873, Twain wrote Hay that he had a putrid anecdote for Hay and was preserving it for a while in alcohol.

In April, the makings of one of those marvelous anecdotes now clustering about the Twain myth occurred, when Charles Dudley Warner and Twain appealed to Reid of the *Tribune* to favor them with a review of their *Gilded Age*. After Reid gave the request to Hay, he promptly wrote and published such a liberal review that even Twain took fright. Reid had to rescue the worried co-authors by publishing a conservative puff.[17] In December, 1874, Hay wrote Twain a revealing tribute after having seen the first installment of "Old Times on the Mississippi": "I have just read with delight your article in the Atlantic. It is perfect—no more nor less. I don't see how you do it. I knew all that, every word of it—passed as much time on the levee as you ever did, knew the same crowd & saw the same scenes,—but I could not have remembered one word of it all. You have the two greatest gifts of the writer, memory & imagination. I congratulate you." When Twain sent a copy of Hay's praise to Howells, he remarked, "Now isn't that outspoken & hearty, & just like that splendid John Hay?"[18]

Early in 1875, Twain tried to get Hay to voyage up and down the Mississippi River with him, to refresh memories that could then go into *Life on the Mississippi*; but Hay pleaded the arrival of the first Hay baby. In October, 1879, Twain querulously wrote Howells: "Hang it, I wish John Hay & his wife would give *us* a call, next time they look in on you."[19] A couple of weeks later Twain wanted Hay, as well as Howells and their ministerial friend Joseph H. Twichell, to descend on Chicago in connection with Twain's celebrated "Babies" speech there in praise of U. S. Grant. But Hay was still too busy, this time with Republican party politics.[20]

Early in 1880, when Twain wrote Howells suggesting the formation of "The Modest Club," he named a few possible members and included Hay, to whom Howells forwarded the proposal. When Hay returned his endorsement, he invited Twain and Howells to come to Washington to "hold the first meeting of three at my house."[21] In June, when Hay got his hands on Twain's manuscript that contained his notorious "1601," he treasured it and wanted to share its delight with a Cleveland friend, probably a fellow Vampire Club member,[22] to whom he sent pseudoserious letters praising the "masterpiece" as "a serious effort to bring back our literature and philosophy to the sober and chaste Elizabethan standard." When the Cleveland friend had had his chance at "1601," he teased Hay with the news that it had been set in type. Hay replied: ". . . the proposition which you make to pull a few proofs of the masterpiece is highly attractive, and of course highly immoral. I cannot properly consent to it. . . . Please send back the document as soon as you can, and if, in spite of my prohibition, you take these proofs, save me one."[23]

When Twain learned of the suicide in May, 1883, of Hay's father-in-law Amasa Stone, he wrote Howells about the irony in the fact that the Hays, happily voyaging home from England, would soon be greeted by the grisly news in New York: ". . . Hay and his wife sailed from Liverpool just in time to escape hearing of the catastrophe. The suicide lies waiting . . . , and these children are still enjoying themselves on the Atlantic, unaware of what is in store for them. How odd and strange and wierd [*sic*] all this is. Apparently nothing pleases the Almighty like the picturesque."[24]

Only minor items concerning Hay's friendship with Twain remain to be mentioned. Twain was undoubtedly not privy to the secret of the authorship of *The Bread-Winners*. However, he wrote an enigmatic postscript to his curious Cleveland correspondent, Mrs. Mary Mason Fairbanks (whom Hay also knew well), the month the novel appeared in book form: "*I* believe John Hay wrote it [title not given], but I don't know." The editor of Twain's letters to Mrs. Fairbanks comments that *The Bread-Winners* is probably the subject of the remark.[25]

Twain's last comment on Hay while he was still alive is also the only unpleasant one. In November, 1904, Twain penned a letter to Twichell in which he criticized Hay for campaigning for Roosevelt. Long though the passage is, it is worth quoting in full:

Oh, dear! get out of that sewer—party politics—dear Joe. At least with your mouth. We had only two men who could make speeches for their parties and preserve their honor and their dignity. One of them is dead. Possibly there were four. I am sorry for John Hay; sorry and ashamed. And yet I know he couldn't help it. He wears the collar, and he had to pay the penalty. Certainly he had no more desire to stand up before a mob of confiding human incapables and debauch them than you had. Certainly he took no more real pleasure in distorting history, concealing facts, propagating immoralities, and appealing to the sordid side of human nature than you did; but he was his party's property, and he had to climb away down and do it.[26]

What had brought Twain's anger to a spluttering head was Hay's policy toward the Philippines and China. Twain's inflexibly anti-imperialistic position is too well known to require elaboration here.

III   *William Dean Howells*

Howells liked almost anyone who could write well; and, early in his life, he paid less attention to his literary friends' politicial predilections than to their stylistic felicities. He therefore had no difficulty with Hay, even though Hay grew more conservative over the years, while Howells became more liberal, especially after the Haymarket Riot in Chicago in 1886. The two men did each other favors before they became friends; each respected the other's life style; and they socialized and even traveled together. Their friendship may be characterized as editorial, esthetic, and formal

rather than either intellectual—like Hay's relationship with
Adams—or informal—like Hay's relationship with Twain.

After Howells had written Lincoln's 1860 campaign biography,
he petitioned, through Nicolay and Hay, for a consular appointment and was soon sent to Venice. Returning home in 1866, he joined
the *Atlantic* staff and five years later was its editor-in-chief. In 1870,
he accepted part of Hay's *Castilian Days* for serial publication. In
December of that year, Hay praised Howells's *Their Wedding
Journey* by letter, wondered whether he had seen Hay's "Little
Breeches," and urged Howells to write a Western novel in a similar
dialect. Hay added, probably with accuracy, "I can't do it—but you
could." Next May, Howells praised *Castilian Days*, which its author
then denied anything comparable to Howells's travel writing.[27] In
November, Howells favorably reviewed in the *Atlantic* Hay's book
on Spain.

In May, 1872, the two men met in New York at *Atlantic* publisher
James R. Osgood's Delmonico dinner. They continued to exchange
letters for some years; Howells tried fruitlessly early in 1877 to in-
duce Hay to write some fiction for the *Atlantic*; and after Hay
began his first Department of State work in 1879, Howells realized
that his friend was more important. He accurately wrote Hay: "You
are a far greater man than that office needs," and the following
summer he urged Hay to use his influence to improve the international copyright laws.[28]

In preparation for a rendezvous in Europe late in 1882, Howells
and Hay exchanged interesting letters in March. For his part,
Howells told of his literary plans and reported that his children had
begun to read his fiction: "For this reason, if for no other, I could
not have palpitating divans in my stories; my children are my cen-
sors, and if I wished to be wicked, I hope they would be my safe-
guards." As for Hay, he lightly wrote Howells that he would "take a
lot of historical notes in my [steamer] trunk, ostensibly to write a
few chapters [in *Lincoln*], but really to ballast me, and lower my
spirits with the thought of duty unperformed."[29] Hay and Howells
were complementary but not kindred spirits.

They saw each other in London in the summer of 1882, and then
in Florence, very early in 1883. Howells wrote Hay informing him
that T. B. Aldrich, then editing the *Atlantic*, "says he will accept
the story [*The Bread-Winners*] unsight and unseen, but he wants
the author's name to go with it!" As we know, Hay refused to
publish his name and let the *Century* serialize it anonymously in-

stead. Later Howells offered Hay genial but hard-hitting criticism of his novel but praised it because it expressed "the fact that the workingmen *as* workingmen are no better or wiser than the rich *as* the rich, and are quite as likely to be false and foolish. It certainly didn't strike me that the author was assailing them as a class."[30]

When they returned to the United States, the two saw little of each other for a few years, nor did they correspond very much. In the significant 1890s, the record becomes even more sparse. In January, 1890, Hay complained to Howells that he was sick of readying *Lincoln* for publication: "I have worked so like a dray-horse of late that I have seen nothing, heard nothing, read nothing; our proof-reading is half over." In June, he wrote Howells, modestly and affectionately, of a project: "I have had the impudence to collect all my verses, new and stale, into one volume which H[oughton] & M[ifflin] have printed. But I have at the same time printed a little edition of them for my friends and lovers, of which I send you a copy. You will not suspect me of taking them too seriously in thus dressing them up. On the contrary, it is only the conscious amateur who does such things." Howells, who habitually repaid kindness with praise, then assured Hay that "I took your revised poems . . . out to Ohio with me. . . . [E]very morning when the birds sang me awake, I lay in bed and read your verse. It seemed to me wonderfully good, passing by far what I used to think of it in my friendliest moments." Then Howells expressed his gratitude for Hay's approval of his *Hazard of New Fortunes,* which liberal novel might have displeased the author of the conservative *Bread-Winners:* ". . . I fancied that it might be farther from your thinking, in some things, than it would be from your feelings. So, What would John Hay say? was among my questions." In 1897, when Howells joined the Century Club, of which Hay, Adams, and Henry James had long been members, Hay most likely played a considerable role in Howells's election.[31]

The records of the early twentieth century yield even less evidence of the continuing close friendship of Hay and Howells, for they grew ever farther apart politically. When Hay wrote his friend in 1903 to lament that distance, he added that "the solitude deepens around me year by year." After Hay's death, Howells published in the *North American Review* his "John Hay in Literature," in which he praised Hay's Ellsworth essay, the ethics of his poetry, his noble *Lincoln,* and his diplomatic acumen. Years later, when Howells first visited Spain, he checked the validity of

Hay's much earlier insistence that the best Titians were at the Prado and not in Venice.[32]

IV   Henry James

The one close literary friendship to be discussed is that which Hay enjoyed with Henry James. Documenting and analyzing their relationship thoroughly, George Monteiro then definitively concludes as follows:

The correspondence of Henry James and John Hay . . . forms the record of a mutually satisfactory friendship, cultivated carefully over thirty years. . . . James's letters are the cordial, considerate, sometimes intimate letters of a patrician artist to a sympathetic friend, one capable of understanding his best work from the point of view of an informed man of public affairs and a fellow American, but not necessarily that of a critic or fellow artist. . . . James did not choose to talk shop at any length or to any depth with Hay. Nor is there evidence . . . of James's having felt the necessity to resort in his relations with Hay to "the mere twaddle of graciousness" . . . that he could summon, when necessary, to puncture someone softly and surely. . . . [W]e can readily locate traces of conscious inflation of the importance of Hay's literary accomplishments. . . . But instances of such "graciousness" are few, although the letters are certainly not devoid of the necessarily careful, but genuine amenities of friendship.[33]

Hay and James may have first met early in 1875, perhaps through their mutual friend Howells. James was then planning to return to Europe for an indefinite stay and wanted to be the New York *Tribune's* Parisian literary correspondent, which Hay helped him to become. He recommended James to Reid, and praised James and his inadequately vulgar letters; but, all the same, the series soon flopped.[34]

During the next quarter of a century, which James spent mostly abroad, largely in London, Hay frequently visited Europe and often saw James in England. James evidently did not think too highly of Clara Hay, for he privately limned her as "big, handsome, *vaccine*." After Osgood gave a big banquet for American writers—including Hay, Howells, and James—in London in September, 1882, James and Hay went separately to France. James gathered impressions for his *Little Tour in France*, but Hay unsuccessfully sought the fountains of youth at Cannes. When the two had a rendezvous in Paris in November, wild Clarence King was also present; they all breakfasted, sauntered, shopped, went to the theater, and talked about literature. Constance Fenimore Woolson wrote to James the following May that Hay had said that, although he revered James and his work, "He cares nothing for me; I have always known it, & it came out again, plainly, in Paris. But I care a great deal for him."[35]

Monteiro, who first published Miss Woolson's upsetting revelation, comments: "Just why Hay should have felt that James had not cared for him remains puzzling, for at that very time James was writing enthusiastically to Howells about Hay's excellence and King's charm."[36] But the plain though deep cause of Hay's unease was surely threefold: he was talking literature with practicing experts but was producing little himself, he had talent but was lolling through Europe on the unearned capital of others, and he was chronically sick.

The Hay-James record is rather skimpy from this point until 1897, when Hay became ambassador to England. In the spring of 1884, in the summer of 1887, and in the spring of 1891, Hay had vacationed in London, had given lavish literary parties, and had always been happy to welcome James to them. Although the two men had missed connections when Hay was abroad in 1893 - 1894, they corresponded, especially in regard to the death of Miss Woolson, whose burial in Rome on January 31, 1894, James had handled.[37] Once he became ambassador, Hay saw James more often, beginning with Hay's first ambassadorial day. James was present at the Southampton pier to welcome his friend, albeit querying him the while: "What impression does it make on your mind to have these insects creeping about and saying things to you?" he wondered.[38]

When Hay and Adams invited the busy novelist to join them on their Nile trip, James declined partly because he had recently leased Lamb House, Rye, in Sussex; but he was able to visit Surrenden Dering in nearby Kent—a monumental manor house leased by Senator James Donald Cameron and his wife Elizabeth.[39] She and Adams were close correspondents. If it is possible—as Leon Edel has suggested—that this estate was the prototype of a similar one in James's disturbing novel *The Sacred Fount,* then it may also be possible that James was probing in only a partially disarming fictive form the interrelationships of the Camerons, the Hays, Adams, and himself at Surrenden.[40]

While Hay was secretary of state, James returned, in August,

1904, to his native land, declined an invitation to visit the vacationing Hays at Lake Sunapee, but did attend a fancy dinner in Washington in early January. Because of Hay's undeviating graciousness, all was sweet and affable in spite of the presence of fellow guest President Roosevelt, who had previously defined James as a snob whose fiction was pointless, and who later blamed Hay's alleged ineffectuality in office on his friendship with people like James and Adams.[41] After this meeting, Hay and James never saw one another again.

James recorded a few opinions of Hay's writing. In 1890, James wrote that he would be happy to accept a copy of Hay's poetry but seems not to have commented later on the contents. He disliked the anonymous *Bread-Winners* and lumped its dismaying popularity with that of *To Leeward* (1883), one of Francis Marion Crawford's many runaway best sellers of the same epoch. He evidently liked Hay's *Lincoln;* he called it an "epic" and also "a wonderful gallery of pictures of the vast democratic American life." Finally, though he sent Henry Adams a bundle of old letters for the projected *Letters of John Hay,* he evidently made no comment about the ensuing volumes. He may have said enough when he wrote Clara Hay on her first Christmas as a widow and commended her late husband—not as a writer but simply as "a very admirable & special friend & appreciator, an exquisite & faithful critic. . . ."[42]

V   *Other Friends*

Among scores of other friends, a few stand out as influential upon Hay the writer. John George Nicolay was foremost. Clarence King's lucky friends, including Hay, treasured his knowledge, smile, laugh, persiflage, energy, and generosity. Whitelaw Reid was Hay's most important editorial contact. Bret Harte was never close to Hay; but the independent appearance of their humorous dialect poetry at about the same time threw their names into conjunction, and the two men later saw each other on occasion. Hay tolerated Harte more than he should have, perhaps because Hay saw in the wandering failure an image of what might happen to a weak-willed man without a good, rich wife. Constance Fenimore Woolson may have first met Hay through their mutual Cleveland friends and relatives; her nephew Samuel Mather married Flora Stone, Hay's wife Clara's sister. Many of Miss Woolson's stories deal with Americans abroad in the manner of Hay and James.[43]

Three other friends of Hay stand out. Richard Watson Gilder was on the editorial staff of *Scribner's Monthly* when in 1881 it became the *Century*, which published Hay's *Bread-Winners* and parts of his and Nicolay's *Lincoln*. As for Carl Schurz, a brilliant, German-born radical who impressed Lincoln as well as young Hay, he and Hay remained friends even though they increasingly differed on national policy over the decades. And Edmund Clarence Stedman, the popular and influential poet and editor who has since gone into eclipse, and Hay were fellow members of the Century Club, the National Institute of Arts and Letters, and the American Academy of Arts and Letters.

Finally, Walt Whitman was one of Hay's best friends. They met ·in Washington early in the Civil War. Later Hay helped Whitman with money and followed his career with surprising fidelity. The Good Gray Poet once recalled: "Hay I knew well: we met often: Hay . . . was a very handsome fellow: good body, open face, easy manners. . . . Hay married a millionairess . . . : he had, however, remained simple, himself, unaffected—and is still my friend."[44]

If we judge people by the company they keep, John Hay must loom uniquely large against the bizarre sky of late nineteenth-century America. He merited Henry Adams's respect, exchanged laughs with Mark Twain, was friendly with William Dean Howells, saw worth in Henry James well before the critics did, and befriended the most robust poet of the century—Walt Whitman. These friends and others may have differed with Hay about questions of substance and style, but all of them agreed that Hay was a cherished comrade.

CHAPTER 4

Hay's Poetry

JOHN Hay's son Clarence once wrote about his father that, "But for the statesman in him, he would have been more a poet; but for the poet in him, he would have been less a statesman"[1]; and the subtitle of Dennett's biography of Hay is *From Poetry to Politics*. The sententious son wrongly implies that Hay was an important poet, and the biographer seems to imply that Hay had to quit writing poetry before he could turn to more serious work. In truth, Hay exercised a genuine but minor poetic talent most of his life, he took his versifying seriously, and a few of his poems were once unbelievably popular.

Hay wrote some rather affected poetry while at Brown University. The Civil War shook a little doggerel out of him. Napoleon III of France and Isabella II of Spain aroused his republican ire. He turned out very pleasant ballads in Pike County dialect. His fiancée Clara—later his wife—stirred him to compose warm though general love lyrics. He also penned some rather vapid religious verse and wrote other minor items from time to time.

I Pike County Ballads

Whether John Hay or Bret Harte first exploited Pike County dialect in tender-tough vernacular ballads is a tepid critical question, which once aroused partisans but which will probably never be answered. Mark Twain, William Dean Howells, and Clarence Hay opined that Hay's Pike County poems were the first; but Clarence King, Sister Saint Ignatius Ward, and perhaps Fred Lewis Pattee believed that Harte's work antedated Hay's.[2] No matter which author was the first to use this dialect, however, such subdialects were popular with local-color writers and their readers.

The six items collected in *Pike County Ballads* are "Jim Bludso," "Little Breeches," "Banty Tim," "The Mystery of Gilgal,"

54

"Golyer," and "The Pledge at Spunky Point." "Jim Bludso," "Little Breeches," "Banty Tim," and "The Pledge," which are in fairly regular ballad form, are presented in eight-line stanzas; the iambic and anapestic tetrameter alternates with trimeter; and the rhyme scheme is *abcbdefe*. "Gilgal" is in four-line stanzas, with iambic and anapestic feet, the first three lines tetrameter and the fourth trimeter, rhyming *aabb*. "Golyer" uses five-line stanzas rhyming *abccb*, with iambic and anapestic feet, all lines being tetrameter but for a trimeter last line; the final stanza has an extra line and rhymes *abcccb*, all lines again being tetrameter but the last one.

What first strikes the modern reader of *Pike County Ballads* is their skillfully employed diction. They sound as though they had been written by an honest, unschooled adult from Twain's *Adventures of Huckleberry Finn*, for the lines of the ballads are regularly peppered with words and phrases such as "reckon," "git," "you 'low," "sh'n't," "Dimocrats," "seein'," "bein'," "out o' j'int," "nigger," "mosey," and "P'int." The ballads present a vague image of the narrator: he is laconic, unemotional, stalwart, humor-loving; he is admirable as a friend; but he is not a man to tangle with. When the narrator becomes Sergeant Tilmon Joy in "Banty Tim," he is more obviously frank and rawboned. The reader finds himself puzzled that Hay, later diplomat *extraordinaire*, could ever have composed these ballads which resemble rude carvings in pinewood much more than they do intricate, delicate oriental art work in porcelain and jade, of the sort that he later admired.

The best Hay ballad, "Jim Bludso," was an instantaneous, nationwide success and the topic of pulpit disapproval. After Mark Twain chided Hay for making his hero Bludso a Mississippi River steamboat engineer instead of a pilot, Hay was troubled for years until the son of Oliver Fairchild, Bludso's model, told him that the original had indeed been an engineer who had died in precisely the manner detailed in the poem. Legend has it that Hay wrote the poem while visiting his parents in Warsaw in the fall of 1870 and while staying in a Keokuk hotel that overlooked the Mississippi River.[3]

Comprehensive aspects of the traditional American creed are succinctly stated in "Jim Bludso": to worship machinery, compete, and respect discipline. Jim, who "passed in his checks / The night of the Prairie Bell,"[4] was "no saint"; he had "One wife in Natchez-under-the-Hill / And another one here, in Pike" (p. 3). But he fought well and never lied, and his only "religion" was "To treat his engine

well; / Never be passed on the river; / To mind the pilot's bell."
During a race with "a better boat," in a scene that Twain may have
had in mind when he wrote chapter 4 of *The Gilded Age*,[5] fire
erupts from the *Prairie Bell*'s furnace. But Bludso—ever mindful of
his promise to "hold her nuzzle agin the bank / Till the last galoot
got ashore" (p. 4)—is the hero in all eyes, when, assuring the safety
of all passengers, he burns to death. The narrator, admitting that his
friend was sinful compared to "pious gentlemen / That would n't
shook hands with him," concludes all the same that

> He seen his duty, a dead-sure thing,—
> And went for it thar and then;
> And Christ ain't a-going to be too hard
> On a man that died for men. (p. 5)

Although these lines offended conservative ministers, they pleased
the multitudes. Hay's poem was widely reprinted and was popular abroad, especially in England. It went into contemporary
anthologies of verse—more than a dozen of them, in fact, by 1905,[6]
the year of the death of Hay, who—without our getting
maudlin—we may say "seen his duty" in 1898, "went for it thar
and then," and gave his life, as Bludso did, "for men."

"Jim Bludso" is the only poem by Hay that, to my knowledge,
has been subjected to detailed modern critical analysis. In the
useful *Art of Reading Poetry*, Earl Daniels reprints the poem, and
praises its commonplace material, predictable action, appropriate
tone, quiet emotionalism, graphic details, and homely phrasing. He
also rightly objects to the false note of its neatly tied moral, and to
its absence both of struggle and of character complexity.[7]

"Little Breeches," which was composed about when "Jim Bludso" was, actually saw print earlier. Hay later revealed that his
source of inspiration for "Little Breeches" had been a sermon he
once heard in the Warsaw Presbyterian Church about "Proudfoot's
little boy in Iowa in 1863."[8] This poem was offensive to the strait-
laced, but it too was immensely popular. Although the narrator first
explains that "I don't go much on religion, / I never ain't had no
show," and that he does not believe in the prophets or free will, he
does "b'lieve in God and the angels, / Ever sence one night last
spring." In the rest of the poem, a homely exemplum, the narrator
goes to town with his son Gabe (also called "Little Breeches"), a
"sassy," lovable four-year-old who has learned to swear and "chaw
terbacker" (p. 6). When the narrator enters a store for molasses, he

leaves little Gabe outside with the team, which spooks and bolts through a snowstorm "hell-to-split over the prairie!" (p. 7). The distraught father and a friend named "Isrul Parr" (p. 8) follow with torches; they find the "hosses and wagon" all "Upsot" (p. 7), but Gabe has disappeared. After the narrator has flopped down "Crotch-deep in the snow" to pray, the men look for the boy in "a little shed / Where [not Whar] they shut up the lambs at night." Little Breeches, safe inside, is stridently calling for his tobacco. After the narrator has concluded that angels "jest scooped down and toted him / To whar [not where] it was safe and warm" (p. 8), he then generalizes:

> And I think that saving a little child,
>   And fotching him to his own,
> Is a derned sight better business
>   Than loafing around the Throne. (p. 9)

Thus summarized, the poem seems neither superb nor theologically unacceptable, but rather tame. Read aloud, however, with a sympathetic voice, the poem is suspenseful, graphic, and moving, if also sentimental and reductive. As for the evidence that the conclusion was quickly pronounced offensive, one contemporary newspaper called it "prostitution of the mission of poetry . . . vulgar doggerel . . . degradation of poetical composition," and even "presumptuous blasphemy."[9]

"Banty Tim" is a dramatic monologue in which Sergeant Tilmon Joy opposes the decision of the racist White Man's Committee of Spunky Point, Illinois, that will not permit the black lad Banty Tim to stay in town. Wounded at Vicksburg Heights and left to be "br'iled and blistered and burned" in the sun while rebel bullets whizzed all around, Tilmon was soon carried to safety by brave Tim, "Till safe in our lines he drapped us both, / His black hide riddled with balls" (p. 12). Tilmon closes with the threat that, though the townsmen "may rezoloot till the cows come home," anyone touching Tim will "wrastle his hash to-night in hell" (p. 13). The lingo may be unsavory, but the point is clear.

In "The Mystery of Gilgal," Hay's most adroit ballad, the callous narrator implies that the mystery he proposes to unfold has to do with reasons behind a murderous fight at Tom Taggart's busy bar in Gilgal. Young Colonel Blood and old Judge Phinn enter, and each calls for a "whisky-skin" at the same time. Tom quickly serves one, the two customers argue over whose it is, and their brutal words

58   JOHN HAY

lead to knives and then guns. The climax may be foreshadowed by
statements indicative of unconcern over sudden death: "They carved
in a way that all admired" (p. 15); then a stray bullet "took Seth
Bludso 'twixt the eyes, / Which caused him great surprise."
Onlookers enter the fight, and soon "They piled the stiffs outside
the door." By now the subject of the puzzle is almost clear. The
narrator closes with the confession that he has "sarched in
vain . . . / But I end with *hit* as I did begin,—"WHO GOT THE
WHISKY-SKIN?" (p. 16).

In "Golyer," which is more sentimental than "Jim Bludso" or
"Little Breeches," Ben Golyer is a typical Western character who is
familiar to the readers of California local-color fiction of a century
ago and to television addicts today: he is a big, ugly, rough
stagecoach driver whose heart of gold is touched by a little orphan
boy who "bawled and kicked and howled" (p. 18) because he wants
to ride on the box with Ben. The man upbraids everyone—including the passenger-narrator—who would dissuade him;
then he tenderly holds the tot, cracks the whip, and off they rattle.
Apaches shoot at them in the night, but Golyer brings them all to
their destination safely. He explains, "When they fired, I kivered
the kid . . . " Then he breathlessly adds, "Although I ain't pretty,
I'm middlin' broad; / And look! he ain't fazed by arrow nor
ball,— / Thank God! my own carcase stopped them all." The
narrator abruptly closes: "And he carried his thanks to God" (p. 20).
No summary can do justice to the clipped characterization and the
effective conclusion. The dialect is well managed, the pace is quick,
and the moral repeats Bludso's message and that of "Little
Breeches": God prefers those who protect the defenseless rather
than those who passively glorify His throne.

The story of "The Pledge at Spunky Point" would have provided
material for a worthwhile five-minute comic interlude in *High
Noon, Shane,* or *Blazing Saddles.* The narrator opens by telling the
Squire to "toddle along with your pledge," because "I've been
thar, / And I'll not take any in mine." Why not? Well, he and a
bunch of the boys last Fourth of July got so corned" (p. 21) that
they signed a year-long temperance pledge and even put up a total
of a hundred dollars for Deacon Kedge to hold for the winner or
winners. One after another, the abstemious turned to drink again.
For example, in March, the Golyers "Got so drunk that a fresh-biled
owl / Would 'a' looked 'long-side o' them two young men, / Like a
sober temperance fowl." Finally, the narrator, who was the sole

contender left for the prize, "... never slep' without dreamin'
dreams / Of Burbin, Peach, or Rye." When the new Fourth of July
at last arrived, he rushed to Taggart's, "For the pledge was off at
noon" (p. 23). His wet cronies who were there with poised glasses
watched him watch the clock thirstily. When it struck twelve, he
took a mighty pull on a jug, only to be stunned by fiendish
laughter: "Them ornery sneaks had sot the clock / A half an hour
ahead!" The narrator would have ordered drinks around and let the
ante pay, but the deacon had just that moment lost it to Parson
Skeeters "In the tail of a game of Draw" (p. 24). The poem has
sustained pace because of the breaking of one pledge after another.
It has unusual images—for example, the one evoked by the "fresh-
biled owl," which is so mocking that it distracts the reader from the
plot. Once again, there is suspense, maybe even surprise.

Pike County Ballads contain Hay's most sustained and memorable body of verse. These poems depict a little world; they sketch a
variety of characters, some of whom reappear in more than one
piece; and the dialect is bracing, credible, and always a bit surprising from Hay. The poems are usually understated. They
dramatize the manly virtues of courage, self-control, and
camaraderie. Together, they comprise a miniscule Tilbury Town -
like cycle; further, Hay shares with E. A. Robinson the ability
simultaneously to smile gently with and to laugh at the foibles of his
very human folk.

II *Other Poems*

In 1890, when Hay gathered into one book all of his poems that
he wished to save, he included several that he should have preferred
to hide. The collection proved popular enough to be reissued during
his lifetime, in 1891, 1892, 1896, 1897, 1899, and 1901; and it has
reappeared since his death. In addition to a section devoted to his
Pike County Ballads, the book features "Wanderlieder" (German,
"songs of wandering"), "New and Old" poems, and a few unimportant "Translations."

Hay's "Wanderlieder" fall into three categories: several concern
European politics, a few deal with love or its absence, and a couple
are fables. Young Hay's diplomatic work in Europe generated some
prorepublican, antidespotic verse, which is surprising in view of his
later conservatism. "Sunrise in the Place de la Concorde" is a
lyrical, first-person tone poem, which is written mostly in trimeter

lines, and which has stanzas of irregular lengths and unpatterned
rhymes. The poet deplores the excesses of the French Revolution
but even more the rule of Napoleon III, who is depicted as "A lurking jail-bird" who has strangled the child of Freedom "As it lay in
his arms asleep" (p. 33). Then, as many of Hay's early poems do,
"Sunrise" ends with a hackneyed dawn image, a note of hope.

"The Sphinx of the Tuileries" compares Napoleon III to the
sphinx that guards the Pavillon de Flore. Both the man and the
statue seem debonair from the front, but both have false paws to be
furtive with and sport "The ignoble form of a craven cur" when
viewed from the rear. Hay inaccurately predicts that when the people, like Oedipus, limp up to this latter-day "bastard Sphinx" (p.
36) and shout his real name, he will lose his power and cringe. The
poem has five stanzas, each of eight lines, rhymes abcbdefe, and has
familiar three- and four-beat lines. Hay might have achieved a
greater degree of sonority and authority if he had used pentameter
more regularly than he did.

"Boudoir Prophecies," a marvelously compressed poem, is only
"apparently playful in tone"—as Sister Ignatius aptly notes[10]—and
effectively suggests that, while Empress Eugénie of France thinks
Queen Isabella II of Spain will soon be in political difficulties, the
queen is thinking the same thing about the empress: "Both ladies,
though not over-wise, / Were lucky in prophecies" (p. 61).[11] The
stanzaic form closely resembles that of "The Sphinx" and has the
identical result: singsong lines that try to carry too heavy a burden.

"A Triumph of Order," the most terrifying of Hay's political
poems, has a title that is bitterly ironic. The days of the Paris Com-
mune rise before us when a little gamin is portrayed as promising a
grizzled infantry captain to return from a domestic errand in time to
be executed with his friends, the captured "rebels / By the wall of
Père-de-Chaise" (p. 63). The boy surprises the squad leader by
keeping his promise; and, in due course, "The Chassepots tore the
stout young heart, / And saved Society." Hay achieved fine irony
when his doomed lad shouts to his manly executioners at the end,
"Now blaze away, my children!" (p. 65).

Vienna inspired Hay to write "The Curse of Hungary." In his
"donjon" (p. 44), old King Salomon curses his land and its people
before he dies: "May a king wrong them as they wrong their king!"
The king's curse affects the eighteenth century just as "the rushing
river / Still brawls by the spot where his donjon stands" (p. 45).
Wily Maria Theresa catches and then chains the loyal, cheated

hearts of her people. In the nineteenth century, Louis Kossuth is ultimately no better. In Hay's own time, it is "But ever the same sad play . . . , / The same weak worship of sword and crown"; and memories of Austro-Russian domination remain vivid. But Hay finds it possible to end, once again, on a note of dawning hope: Salomon's donjon still stands, to be sure, "But Time is crumbling its battered towers; / And the slow light withers a despot's [presumably Francis Joseph's] powers, / And a mad King's curse is not forever!" (p. 46). Although Hay's poem may once have had power, its imagery of clouds and fetters is now trite; and its dated references condemn it to the category of undusted occasional verse.[12]

Next on Hay's itinerary was Spain, which yielded not only *Castilian Days* but some poetry, "The Surrender of Spain." Less than a year before Hay arrived in Madrid, Queen Isabella II had been expelled; the subsequent efforts to establish a republic failed, and monarchical parties under army control soon persuaded Prince Amadeus of Savoy to take the throne. In his poems, Hay scornfully rebuked Spain: "Now to the upstart Savoyard thou bendest to beg for a master! / How the red flush of her shame mars the proud beauty of Spain!" (p. 39). Yet again, however, Hay ends on an assonant note of hackneyed hope: "Once again will she rise, flinging her gyves in the sea!" (p. 40).

Another political poem to be mentioned here is "The Prayer of the Romans," in which Hay rehearses in staccato lines the gory history of Italy up through the Risorgimento—led by the "Lame Lion of Caprera [Giuseppe Garibaldi]!"—to the year 1871, which has not yet quite seen "Liberty and . . . Light" and which cannot do so until "crosier and crown pass away" (p. 42).[13] Then will emerge "One freedom, one faith without fetters, / One republic in Italy free!" (p. 43).

Like Hay's bookishly martial republican strophes, his love poetry also smacks more of the library than of experience. Still, some of it is rather fine. The best early example is "My Castle in Spain," in which Hay adumbrates with Coleridgean, Poe-like lushness an image of a sumptuously appointed castle, for which, however, his heart does not sigh:

> 'Tis the pearl gives worth to the shell—
>   The pearl I would die to gain;
>   For there does my lady dwell,

> My love that I love so well—
> The Queen whose gracious reign
> Makes glad my Castle in Spain. (p. 72)

He mainly thinks of her "honest eyes" and "dear feet" (p. 72)[14] as he is climbing the hill toward the castle where all "Unconscious she waits for me" (p. 73). The versification of this poem is more ingenious than usual. Its six stanzas vary in length from nine to fourteen lines (usually trimeter), with three to six rhymes—usually simple ones such as "Spain," "plain," "pain," "gain" (p. 70).

  Hay often poetizes on the subject of unhappy or incomplete love. "A Woman's Love," engagingly written in pentameter triplets and once quite popular,[15] tells of a woman in purgatory who is restless because her lover, still alive, must be sad; granted leave to discover his real situation, she flies off—only to find another woman now "curl[ing] his hair and kiss[ing] him" (p. 58).

  In "Ernst of Edelsheim," Hay rings a clever change on the hoary archetype of the scaly dragon mistress; for Ernst finds a cool maiden "couched in moss and moonlight" (p. 66), and soon bears her away to "his towers, / And . . . love and laughter" (p. 67). Alas, at sunrise she tearfully confesses, "I'm half the day a woman, / A serpent half the day" (p. 68). Unabashed, stout Ernst settles for the better half and soon becomes "The happiest of . . . lovers" with "his bride thrice dowered" because "His true love was a serpent / Only half the time!" (p. 69). If in Hay's work, as Howells once wrote, "the prevalent note is that of a morality severe almost to austerity,"[16] we may be entitled to see two morals in "Ernst of Edelsheim": one is to be contented with what love one has, and—more nearly universally—to accept Manicheanism.

  What can be concluded from a careful scrutiny of Hay's "On Pitz Languard" is anybody's guess, for this puzzling poem offers a Hawthornean situation in which three disembodied but shadowy voices whisper on an Alpine crag. The first loved a girl who loved him not; the second loved a woman who loved him but married elsewhere; but the third then announces:

> I loved two girls, one fond, one shy,
> And I never divined which one loved me.
> One married, and now, though I can't tell why,
> Of the four in the story I count but three. (p. 60)

The final stanza reports that, after the three voices have whispered low, "only one shadow scarred the snow" (p. 60) as the narrator

descends. Is the third person now out of love, hence free? Is he uniquely mortal? Did he kill? Did his message help the first two or
help the narrator? Did the "One [who] married" marry the
narrator? The haunting poem also taunts.

A couple of Hay's "Wanderlieder" are fables. The more effective
one is a conventionally cast, popular ballad called "The Enchanted
Shirt," in which to save his own life, a wise doctor tells his self-
indulgent, ailing king that he will recover only when he *sleeps one
night / In the Shirt of a Happy Man*" (p. 53). Couriers ride out
frantically in search of such a shirt, but the only happy fellow they
can locate is shirtless. The news shames and then cures the selfish
monarch, whose "land was glad" (p. 56) at once thereafter.[17] The
didactic little nugget hiding in the dross of the tedious fable called
"Monks of Basle" is that monkish men are wrong to fear that the
devil sings from a bird's throat. Truly, it is recorded, "He has no
ears for Nature's voice / Whose soul is the slave of creed" (p. 51).

The forty-six poems in the "New and Old" section include only a
few that show much development in Hay as a poet. The topics
covered include love, philosophy, war, nature, and miscellaneous
ones; and, in addition to his familiar ballad form, Hay tried some
terza rima, a little blank verse, and a couple of sonnets. The twenty
poems that concern love are usually too rational, too little
passionate; but they are sometimes querulous or stoical. Occasionally, they are neatly turned and clever. "Christine" seems too arctic,
with "Her crown of virgin snow" (p. 86). "The Light of Love" is
skillfully constructed, with sunlight, moonlight, and starlight
successively reminding the thoughtful persona of his lofty, serene,
mysterious object of adoration. In "The White Flag," which is
charming, its persona has sent his beloved a red rose and a white
one; when she wears the white, he thinks she is cold until her words
whisper of surrender.[18] "Remorse" laments that ". . . the saddest
wail is for the lips that died / With the virgin dew upon them" (p.
133). "In the Firelight" is a tender salute to Clara Hay's charms;
but its imagery is neither rhetorically fresh nor sufficiently amorous,
and these lines about the millionairess seem almost ludicrous today:
". . . from our thoughtless Paradise / All care and toil dwelt far
away" (p. 144). "Love's Doubt" recovers nicely, pointing out that
one's memory of love is repeatedly improved upon repetitions of
blissful reality. "A Phylactery" recommends setting "the white
Death's Head on the board" as a *memento mori;* for, since time is
fleeting, men are rightly reminded to "Love well! love truly! and
love fast!" (p. 177). "Regardant" is anemic: the persona lies at his

girl's "firm small feet," madly kisses her girdle, and leaves in due time; but later he is to be damned by the falsity of his "thought that you loved me all the while" (p. 187).

Hay's religious poems were once more popular than they ever should have been. "Mount Tabor," "Religion and Doctrine," "Sinai and Calvary," "The Vision of St. Peter," and "Israel" now seem vapid and general in their commonplace expression of the poet's preference for the spirit of Christ over the letter of any old law. When Hay recommends at the end of "Israel" the "use of the strength that is in you, / . . . wrestling of soul and of sinew" (p. 130), as a means of earning God's blessing, we instantly see why Henry Adams registered his dissatisfaction with the poem.[19] Far better are Hay's nontheological exhortations like those contained in his sonnet "Esse Quam Videri" (Latin, "to be rather than seem"), "Lagrimas" ("I pray for tears as in his parching land / The husbandman for rain," p. 170),[20] and several of his almost Melvillean "Distichs" in their difficult dactyllic hexameters.

Hay's essentially nonreligious, personally philosophical position is sufficiently implied in his once-popular poem "The Stirrup Cup," which was written a quarter of a century before his death, but in which he suggests that, since his "short and happy life is done," "the Pale Horse" of death at his door only "Sound[s] dreadful" as it waits "To bear me forth to unknown lands" (p. 98).

Since Hay saw little of war at close range, he should not have written about it: he did not do so well. "Miles Keogh's Horse" would urge us to believe that honoring the sole, four-legged survivor of General George Custer's massacre "Shall prove to a callous people / . . . the sense of a soldier's worth" (p. 80)! Hay's "Crows at Washington" have their somber beauty, but Herman Melville's swallows over Shiloh are more enduring. Hay's "When the Boys Come Home" is a boy-scout ditty when set beside Walt Whitman's "Reconciliation." Hay's longest military poem is his embarrassing "Guy of the Temple," which is about a formerly lovesick, conscience-stricken crusader who, in more than three hundred blank-verse lines, expresses the hope that he can climb the ladder of love to heaven by being killed at Acre. "Guy" is redeemed by some nicely cadenced archaic imagery, good assonance, pleasant alliteration, and italicized Ave Maria strophes; but it is mortally redolent of Sir Walter Scott.

Hay loved nature in her Wordsworthian rather than her Byronic moods, and he should have expressed that fact in more of his

poetry. His "Prairie" is almost as effective as William Cullen
Bryant's slightly similar but more profound poem. And "On the
River" reminds us of what it is easy to forget: that Hay shared a
Mississippi Valley childhood with the likes of Tom Sawyer and
Huck Finn.

Of his several items of miscellaneous or occasional verse, only "A
Dream of Bric-a-Brac" rises above the level of his weak college
poems. In it the narrator dreams that his "jinrikishaw" down below
"Fusi-yama" (p. 99) drops him off at a shop, which is run by a lithe,
demure girl—"So full was she of Orient grace, / From her slant
eyes and burnished face / Down to her little golden-bronze feet"
(p. 102). She shows him exquisite art objects until "A throng of
tourists filled the place" (p. 104). Their noisy advent gives Hay a
chance to reveal not only his descriptive powers but also some ingrained prejudices: a German countess has a pug dog on a blue-
string leash and also "a fiery face," which contrasts with a nice
English woman's "Cheeks of rose." Worse is the following: "Paddy
from Cork with baggage light / And pockets stuffed with dyna-
mite . . ." (p. 105). The loud tourists look about them and guffaw
at everything, point at the narrator, and then disappear. He asks the
lithe maiden who her friends are, to which she answers flatly, "This
audience is disclosed, . . . / Whenever a man makes a fool of
himself" (p. 106). Part of "A Dream of Bric-a-Brac" anticipates
Vachel Lindsay's somewhat more effective "Chinese Nightingale."

III   *Posthumous Verse*

In Clarence Hay's 1916 edition of his father's *Complete Poetical
Works,* two narrative poems, twenty-one sonnets, nine songs and
lyrics, and a useless item labeled "Rhymes" are preserved under the
rubric of "Uncollected Pieces." These pieces are uneven in quality
and, when considered together, add little to the reputation of Hay
the poet. The titular hero of "Benoni Dunn" rehearses in inap-
propriate ballad form his thesis that "Everything works contráry"
(p. 226), says that "you starve ef you keep the Command-
ments, / And hang ef you break the law" (p. 227), and—somewhat
like a few of E. A. Robinson's later failures—keeps on scowling,
hating, and loafing. "After You, Pilot," a Scott-like ballad,
celebrates brave Commander Tunis A. M. Craven of the *Tecumseh,*
doomed at Mobile Bay, August 5, 1864, during the Civil War. He
let his pilot escape from the smashed turret and went down himself

instead. The diction is operatic; the description, wooden; the emotion, fulsome.[21]

Hay's late sonnets, all in Italian form, betray his easy contentment with the traditional and contain little of substantive value. One dedicated to Theodore Roosevelt prematurely praises the leader's "eye to see the humor of the game, / The scorn of lies, the large Batavian mirth . . ." (p. 232). The title "Twilight on Sandusky Marsh" is less promising than the pleasantly descriptive lines following it. "Sorrento" tries; but it would have been better if Hay had written frank lines on the glorious sunset, rather than pseudoclassical ones about "frolic joy," "syrens," and "the tumultuous laughter of the sea" (p. 235). "Paestum" makes this Keatsian point: "Beauty and truth . . . / . . . force the tribute of the vassal years" to "crumbling loveliness" (p. 236).[22]

"Thanatos Athanatos" (Greek, "deathless death") praises athletes and soldiers who die young, is effective, but is also stodgy in places. "Night in Venice" has amorous assonance, especially in the lines "when from the still lagoon / We glided noiseless through the dim canal" (p. 238), and is one of Hay's most ardent love poems. In "Love's Dawn," another love poem, Hay again employs a trite dawn image—one of his everlasting tropes—to express rapture at seeing his love requited as "Love's morning, glorious, [arises] in her tranquil eyes" (p. 240). "A Challenge" has possibilities but finally presents yet another anemic lover who hopes that death will find him down there kissing his queen's feet. "Obedience" is clever: since she tells him not to love her, he will obey, and love instead only her shoes, gloves, dress, and whatever all those items "clasp, and cling to, and caress" (p. 244)! "Estrella" reveals metrical control but also an ignorance of astronomy. And so they go—all are technically acceptable, even suave at times; all are well patterned intellectually, but usually the emotional charge is of little voltage.

Hay's "Songs and Vespers" are no different. Some are sincere, mildly moving, instructive. For example, "Thy Will Be Done" advocates accepting God's will so aggressively and so cooperatively that it almost makes men and women partners with Him in shaping the divine plan. "Eros Ephemeris" (Greek, "shortlived 'Love' ") suits old Hay better; in it, passion is spent, and we find a Joycean lyric whose two stanzas have the visible shape of goblets—probably empty. The third line of "Sweetest and Dearest" names the categories of most of Hay's similes and metaphors:

> Vain are all names
> To express what thou art,
> Gem, rose, or morning-star,
> Joy of my heart. (p. 262)

The lovers in "Two on the Terrace" commendably hope, against a
backdrop of Washington's Capitol by moonlight, that "future
lovers . . . / On far-off nights like this, / . . . Shall meet, clasp
hands, and kiss" (pp. 265 - 66), even—as Secretary Hay adds
ominously—if the backdrop has crumbled.

IV *Coda*

At its best, Hay's poetry is intellectually alert and is obviously the
product of a powerful mind. Logical, suspenseful and surprising,
sincere, his poetry is what we might neutrally label interesting. But
over the years Hay seldom rose to the high level reached in a few of
his early efforts. Increasingly, the results betray his bookishness, his
cloying didacticism, his generalized or otherwise inadequate passion, his insufficient attention to detail, and his unwillingness to ex-
periment with new forms and new topics.

So, the poetic flame, never very strong in Hay, subsided rather
than leaped over the years; in fact, it occasionally sputtered, only to
be ignored in the rush of more immediate pragmatic and social concerns. But even if Hay had not turned to diplomacy, he would not
have become a great poet, since his literary interests and talents lay
more in prose—in travel essays, fiction, and biography.

CHAPTER 5

Castilian Days

IN the year Hay spent in Spain—from July, 1869, to June, 1870—he performed nominal duties as legation secretary; observed the messy political scene in the Spanish parliament (called the Cortes) that existed after the revolution which deposed Isabella II; became friendly with Republican party spokesman Emilio Castelar y Ripoll and a few other liberals; studied Spanish history with appalled fascination; traveled a little; and wrote letters and diary entries—and the papers, as he called them, that became *Castilian Days*. The last two chapters and then the first five chapters of the book were published in the *Atlantic*, in 1870 and early 1871. The book appeared in September, 1871, only four months after the publication of the contriversial *Pike County Ballads*. *Castilian Days* was also upsetting to some, particularly certain politicians and theologians; but Hay capitalized on the stir by publishing, from June, 1872, through October, 1875, in *Harper's Magazine*, his translation of Castelar's *Republican Movement in Europe*.

Castilian Days enjoyed fine sales. In its first dozen years, it went through six editions, was slightly revised for a popular 1890 edition, and in 1903 reappeared in an abridged volume with beautiful illustrations by Joseph Pennell. By this time the author's formerly rigid bias against "the union of crozier and sceptre"[1] was somewhat relaxed by the excision in this edition of the political chapters—"A Field-Night in the Cortes," "The Moral of Spanish Politics," "The Bourbon Duel," and "Necessity of the Republic." The 1903 edition also omitted both "An Evening with Ghosts," a dull section on spiritualism in Spain, and "Proverbial Philosophy," a charming essay. This diluted edition embarrassed President Roosevelt when a New York Catholic editor sought to ban from the public libraries Hay's Spanish essays—and his poetry to boot—because of their alleged blasphemy.[2]

I   *Table of Contents*

Castilian Days is a disunified, absorbing collection of seventeen essays about Spanish customs, living habits, cities, history, art and museums, religious beliefs, and politics. Hay is knowledgeable, observant, and witty; and he is at his best when he describes cities, castles, museums, scenery, and active Spaniards. As an art critic and student of Spanish architecture, he is adept. He knows Spanish history and dramatizes some of its more lurid episodes with verve. But he is less attractive when, patently writing for the folks at home, he strikes a Yankee posture and contrasts New World freedom of religion and ballot, and freedom from conscription, with the Old World's "triple curse of crown, crozier, and sabre" (p. 292).

Travel writers, like autobiographers, are of two types: those who wish to vivify processes of personal enlightenment and those who prefer to sermonize on the assumption that they are already experienced and know best. In *Castilian Days*, Hay is alternately one and then the other: part of the time, he shares his delight in new experiences and employs narrative devices skillfully; but at other times he converts too many pages into lectures against monarchism, inquisitorial religion, and political corruption.

"Madrid al Fresco" is a curious opening chapter, the point of which is that Madrid lacks tradition[3] and has a large foreign population, an inferior high society, women who are tougher and better built than men, picturesque streets and parks, and violent contrasts in the weather. In this presentation, Hay strikes his initial tone of mockery and sarcasm, the tone that dominates the book. In "Spanish Living and Dying"—in which Hay discusses home life in Spain, family customs, belief in miracles, attitudes of servants, lack of education for women, the ineptness of physicians, and customs surrounding death—his anti-Catholicism begins to appear. "Influence of Tradition in Spanish Life" has as its rigid thesis the truism that irrational devotion to both an autocratic theology and an autocratic monarch has put the Spanish mind in a devilish vise—one that makes spiritual and political evolution almost impossible. Hay's fixed assumption is that where Anglo-Saxons and Spaniards differ, the former are more enlightened. In "Tauromachy," Hay freshly rehearses the tired terms of something anathema to most Anglo-Saxons, the Spanish bullfight; and his style is vivid and effective. In "Red-Letter Days," Hay chronologically presents Spanish holidays—mostly religious ones—beginning in

early May and ending with the Carnival season, Lent, and Easter.
Marred by Hay's predictable prejudice, this section ends with a
lovely vernal touch. Three of these sections—"Spanish Living and
Dying," "Red-Letter Days," and "Tauromachy"—appeared as
parts II, III, and V of *Castilian Days* in the *Atlantic* in 1871.

These five first chapters form a unit that presents Spanish
traditions against the backdrop of Madrid. The next five chapters
comprise another unit, this one concerning a museum, a castle, a city, a palace, and an art form—but Hay arranges these topics with
no discernible logic or movement.

"An Hour with the Painters" provides a careful tour of the
fabulous Prado in Madrid, but to do justice to its unique collection
of paintings by Murillo, Giordano, Raphael, Titian, Veronese,
Teniers, Rubens, Velazquez, Ribera, Van Dyck, Pantoja, Morales,
Juan de Juanes, Andrea del Sarto, Dürer, and Claude would require
weeks of study. The subject permits Hay to show himself as well
prepared, observant, witty and ironic, and enamored of youth,
hospitality, and kindness. "A Castle in the Air" is a graphic digres-
sion on La Granja, the dreamy pile that Philip V built north of
Madrid in the Guadarrama Mountains, and which is so boring that
Hay left it for a side trip to Segovia with its Roman aquaducts and
few tourists. In "The City of the Visigoths," Toledo, Hay provides a
wandering tour, with close-up, personal, narrative accounts balanced pleasantly against sketches featuring historical and architectural data. "The Escorial" pictures the incredible mausoleum,
monastery, palace, and school that Philip II built a few miles
northwest of Madrid in obedience to an order from his father
Charles I.[4] Although the place has plenty to detain the dispassionate
tourist, Hay is so biased that he can hardly separate the information
from his guidebooks and his own observations. The result is a bitter
essay on the dark side of Spanish Catholicism that is written with
sarcasm, with chilly rhetoric, and—once again—with skillful
counterpoint, this time a contrast of icy interiors with warmer, more
pleasant outdoor scenes. In "A Miracle Play," in which Hay offers a
short, vivid description of the Lenten drama of *Mary's Seven
Sorrows*, he combines accurate details, a supercilious nod at
audience naïveté, and rhetorical sneers in indirect defense of Anglo-
American Protestantism and political liberalism.

The next three sections have no substantive unity and are also uneven in quality. "An Evening with Ghosts," the weakest chapter in
the whole book, has to do with spiritualism in Spain and dilates on

Spanish gullibility.[5] "Proverbial Philosophy," a neatly organized essay on Spanish proverbs, covers a multitude of lively topics and does
so vividly. "The Cradle and Grave of Cervantes," which first
appeared as part IV in the *Atlantic* sequence, is a long, splendid
treatment of Spain's one indisputable literary genius. In this essay,
Hay is almost entirely pleasant for a change: he thoroughly enjoyed
visiting areas hallowed by Cervantes's footsteps, and he almost entirely avoids antireligious and antimonarchical pronouncements.

The last four parts of *Castilian Days* are devoted to contemporary
politics. As such, they are unified; but they might have been
omitted from the book without much loss, despite the fact that "A
Field-Night in the Cortes" is dramatic and valuable journalism, and
that "The Bourbon Duel" would make a good old-fashioned
Hollywood scenario. "A Field-Night in the Cortes," Hay's first
signed *Atlantic* selection about Spain, reports in detail a debate held
on the night of March 19, 1870, at the Session Chamber of the
Constituent Cortes, Madrid. The subject was finances, and the
debaters included the entire political spectrum: Prim,[6] Topete,
Rivero, Figuerola, Echegaray, Rios, Becerra, Figueras, Rosas,
Silvela, Valera, Lopez de Ayala, and Hay's republican hero
Castelar. Hay devoted boundless energy in presenting, as an immortal moment of history, an episode essentially transitory. In "The
Moral of Spanish Politics," which comes next in order, Hay again
lays bare his old hatreds—monarchism coupled with Catholicism,
political corruption, and slavery—and he ventures to predict that
the future will be uncertain for Spaniards, even though they are
manageable and individually honorable. "The Bourbon Duel," a
breath of exciting air near the stale end of the book, narrates the
March, 1870, duel between the Duke of Montpensier and his un-
lucky cousin, Prince Henry of Bourbon.[7] Finally, "Necessity of the
Republic" delineates the advantages of establishing a Spanish
republic by showing the miseries of the only two viable alter-
natives—an absolute monarchy and a constitutional monarchy.

II *Main Subjects*

In his *Castilian Days*, Hay found it almost impossible to separate
the church from the state in Spain because he saw them as sym-
biotic demons there. He writes of "the twin despotism of the
Church and the King" (p. 60) and "the concubinage of the spiritual
and temporal power" (p. 70); he deplores the fact that all the Prado

paintings are "held by the clenched dead hand of the church and the throne" (p. 127); and he argues that "the grasping and greedy clergy ran coupled with the tyrant state, and shared the spoil of the robberies it assisted and condoned" during "centuries of despotism" (p. 349).

Almost to a man, Catholic ecclesiasts are useless in Hay's book. St. Ildefonso is not to be believed; and San Isidro—"the ploughboy patron of Madrid" (p. 100)—is a "lazy lout" and a "toady" whose chores the angels did for him in the good old days and whose "bones have done more extensive and remarkable miracle-work than any equal amount of phosphate in existence" (p. 101). The Moors in bygone times were hygienic; but "The monks, who were too lazy to bathe, taught their followers to be filthy by precept and example" (p. 55). Jesuits have exercised a "degrading influence" (p. 179) on church architecture. Hay bestows unique words of praise on Cardinal Ximenez de Cisneros, called "great" (p. 192) for permitting the Moors the free exercise of their religion in Toledo and for restoring, in spite of Alfonso VI's wishes, the ancient Christian liturgy there. Hay also admires Ximenez for liberalizing the University of Alcalá de Henares. In addition, Hay grudgingly lauds the historian-monks of Cervantes's time for their "accurate records" (p. 297).

In like manner, Hay treats Spanish kings and queens. He sarcastically states his firm opinion: "It must be confessed this institution of monarchy is a luxury that must be paid for" (p. 135). Although Ferdinand and Isabella (who reigned 1479 - 1504) are almost ignored, Hay mentions that from their time until that of their great-grandson Philip II there occurred "that wonderful series of reigns . . . which in less than a century raised Spain to the summit of greatness and built up a realm on which the sun never set" (p. 62). Concerning Isabella herself, Hay is content to add only that she "would fain have abolished bathing and bull-fighting together" (p. 75).

Charles I (reigned 1516 - 1556) receives, however, detailed treatment. He is praised as "a munificent protector of art" (p. 122), especially of Titian paintings; but his devoutness is scorned and his infamous Hapsburg blood is unfavorably compared to that of the houses of Castile and Aragon.

Against that monarch's son Philip II (1556 - 1598), Hay unleashes his special rage and invective. From the outset, Philip was no soldier: during the battle of St. Quentin, "this young and chivalrous monarch was beating his breast and pattering his panic-stricken prayers" (p. 213). But he could order others to their death: his "delirious dream that God's wrath was breathing through him upon a revolted [i.e., Protestant] world" was so recurrent that "After only ten years of burnings and beheadings Philip II. could boast that not a heretic lived in his borders" (p. 63).[8] He was a "crazy relic-hunter" (p. 191) who in a "long life of osseous enthusiasm . . . collected seven thousand four hundred and twenty-one genuine relics, . . . sometimes by a miracle of special grace getting duplicate skeletons of the same saint" (p. 220). Hay rightly regards the Escorial, the construction of which Philip II commissioned and supervised, as that monarch's most tangible accomplishment: "So powerful is the influence of a great personality that in the Escorial you can think of no one but Philip II. He lived here only fourteen years, but every corridor and cloister seems to preserve the souvenir of his sombre and imperious genius" (pp. 224 - 25). When Philip II learned about his profligate but devout son Don Carlos's patricidal plan, he "shut him up until he died, in an edifying frame of mind, and then calmly superintended the funeral arrangements from a window of the palace" (p. 226). When Philip II finally died, "The common people mourned him . . . with genuine unpaid sobs and tears. They will weep even yet at the story of his edifying death,—this monkish vampire breathing his last with his eyes fixed on the cross of the mild Nazarene, and tormented with impish doubts as to whether he had drunk blood enough to fit him for the company of the just!" (p. 64). Nor is he entirely forgotten: "In the fine portrait by Pantoja, of Philip in his age, . . . is the face of a living corpse; of a ghastly pallor, heightened by the dull black of his mourning suit, where all passion and feeling has died out of the livid lips and the icy eyes" (p. 133).

Philip III (1598 - 1621), who is said to have had a "booby face" (p. 24), is then described as weakly giving governmental control to the Duke of Lerma; but he is finally characterized as "a monster of cruelty, who burned Jews and banished Moors, not from malice, but purely from vacuity of spirit." He too is immortalized in the incomparable Velazquez's Prado portrait, "pine-apple" head, "plump jowls" (p. 134), and all.

Philip IV (1621 - 1665) is spared more than a touch of Hay's Twainesque sarcasm, as are the later Spanish monarchs. But the author, unable to resist reporting that Philip IV saw fit to open the coffin of Charles I, cannot help adding that it would have been unlikely that anyone opened Philip's: "He stayed above ground too long as it was, and it is probable that people have never cared to look upon his face again. All that was human had died out of him years before his actual demise, and death seemed not to consider it worth while to carry off a vampire" (p. 223). Also frozen in Velazquezian pigment are the features of this "last true king of the old school" (p. 226)—"The high, narrow brow, long, weak face, the yellow curled mustache, the thick red lips, and the ever lengthening Hapsburg chin" (p. 134).

Hay rapidly comes to a temporary end of the line. Charles II (1665 - 1700) struck Hay as a "devil-haunted idiot" (p. 220). Philip V (1700 - 1746) is celebrated for having built La Granja and for having stopped bullfighting in Spain, though only briefly. Ferdinand VI (1746 - 1759) encouraged his subjects to swear loyalty to his baby daughter by having a festival in which ninety-nine bulls were killed. Charles III (1759 - 1788) earns high marks as "the only real ruler the Bourbons ever gave to Spain . . . , and to him Madrid owes all that it has of architecture and civic improvement" (p. 3). Charles IV (1788 - 1808) escapes the pen of Hay, who, however, gives Ferdinand VIII (1808 - 1833) an indirect compliment: his royal stupidity in wanting French wallpaper in his palace resulted in his shipping priceless paintings to the empty Prado museum; he thereby saved them. Hay prematurely concluded that because Isabella II (1833 - 1868) had fled across the Pyrenees, the divine right of Spanish monarchs would be doomed.

Early in *Castilian Days*, Hay describes the new republican party of Spain as "only a year or two old, but what a vigorous and noisy infant it is!" (p. 73). Later in his book, however, a note of worry creeps in: "If this Republican party of yours cannot do something to free Spain from the triple curse of crown, crozier, and sabre, then Spain is in doleful case" (p. 292). Not all of the ingenious logic of his final chapter, "Necessity of the Republic," could prevent a return of the Bourbons—beginning with Alfonso XII—after Castelar's republican government (1873 - 1874) had collapsed.

The Castilian buildings Hay admired most include the following structures in Segovia, with their touches of the Roman, Gothic, and Moorish: "the beautiful votive church of San Juan de los Reyes" (p. 200), San Cristo de la Vega, San Cristo de la Luz, the Military College of Santa Cruz, and the Royal Alcázar, all in Toledo; and the University of Alcalá de Henares. The royal pile that drew his finest ire is the Escorial—"the most cheerless monument in existence" (p.

216) and "an incubus on the breast of earth." In true Yankee fashion, Hay offers Escorial statistics: The place measures 744 feet by 580 feet, and has 11,000 windows. He added, incorrectly, that "it is built, by order of the fantastic bigot [Philip II], in the form of St. Lawrence's gridiron" (p. 217).[9]

A pleasant highlight is Hay's Prado chapter, the longest in his book, which has the unity of an organized lecture tour through the picture galleries that Hay sweepingly defines as "the finest in the world" (p. 121).[10] Hay digresses into the history of painters and paintings, and also pauses to gossip about the backgrounds, usually unsavory, of several of the portrait painters' subjects. In general, Hay prefers artists to patrons, foreign artists to Spanish ones, and ugly, truthful portraits to official ones. His favorite non-Spanish painters in the Prado are Raphael, Rubens, Tintoretto, Titian, Van Dyke, and Veronese. His favorite Spanish painters are Murillo and Velazquez—Murillo for his variety, his sincerity, and especially the details of his *Holy Family*; Velazquez, for a hundred reasons, including his compassion as well as the genius resulting in *The Surrender of Breda, Los Borrachos,* and *Las Meninas,* all of which Hay analyzes in detail and with esthetic common sense. To Hay, *The Surrender of Breda* is "probably the most utterly unaffected historical painting in existence" (p. 142). As for *Los Borrachos,* "These topers have come together to drink, for the love of the wine,—the fun is secondary" (p. 145). In regard to *Las Meninas,* Hay observes that "if art consist in making a fleeting moment immortal, if the True is a higher ideal than the Beautiful, then it will be hard to find a greater painting than this. It is utterly without beauty; . . . yet in its austere fidelity to truth it stands incomparable in the world" (p. 144). According to Hay, a similar fidelity informs Velazquez's best royal portraits. But he does not much like his third-ranking Spanish painter, Ribera, whose immoralities in Naples are deplored; yet Hay does curtly acknowledge the painter's "tumultuous power and energy" (p. 146). Hay has one artist *bête noire,* the unfortunate Italian Giordano, whose slapdash technique caused the author to nickname him "Luca Fa Presto," "Luke Work-Fast," and the "Quick-worker," especially when—at the Escorial—"the nimble Neopolitan . . . [was] emptying his buckets of paint on the ceiling of the grand staircase" (p. 221).

Bad politicians and toadying artists cannot spoil the Spanish landscape for anyone, not even Hay, who should have spent more time and ink in celebrating it. His finest natural description was evoked when, on his way by mule-drawn diligence to La Granja and its affectations, darkness overtook the party:

The quick twilight fell as we entered a vast forest of pines that clothed the mountain side. The enormous trees looked in the dim evening light like the forms of the Anakim, maimed with lightning but still defying heaven. Years of battle with the mountain winds had twisted them into every conceivable shape of writhing and distorted deformity. I never saw trees that so nearly conveyed the idea of being the visible prison of tortured Dryads. their trunks, white and glistening with oozing resin, added to the ghostly impression they created in the uncertain and failing light. (p. 167)

Toledo from a distance inspired Hay, as well as El Greco before him: "The sun was throned, red as a bacchanal king, upon the purple hills, as we descended the rocky declivity and crossed the bridge of St. Martin. . . . We rested on the further side and looked back at the towering city, glorious in the sunset, its spires aflame, its long lines of palace and convent clear in the level rays, its ruins softened in the gathering shadows, the lofty bridge hanging transfigured over the glowing river" (p. 203 - 04). Incidentally, Hay was no exception to the usual nineteenth-century art commentator relative to the tardily discovered virtues of the famous painter of Toledo's skyline, El Greco; for, according to Hay, this "wild Greek bedouin" "filled the walls of convents with his weird ghost-faces" (p. 124) and his Escorial portraits are "weird plague-stricken faces, all chalk and charcoal" (p. 222).

An art critic today, with his obvious advantages, might find fault with Hay's "Hour with the Painters" for slighting Alonso Cano, Alonso Coello, Del Mazo, Esteban March, Ribera, and certainly Goya and Zurbarán. With his antimonarchical bias, Hay may have read too much evil into certain royal portraits. But he rightly slurred over Tiepolo, and he seized upon the works of Murillo and Velazquez with an unerring eye. He was fortunate in being stationed in Madrid and thus having access to the Prado, as were later American tourists who found their strolls through the Prado more enjoyable because of Hay's careful chapter about its masterpieces.

III *Hay's Style*

The four most notable aspects of literary style displayed in *Castilian Days* are Hay's acute powers of observation, his sarcastic wit, his imagery, and his crisp epithets; less admirable are his occasional compositional infelicities. The ordinary objects in the Madrid streets Hay observes and notes in vivid word pictures. For example, he presents the colorful seller of water, "with his brown blouse, his short breeches, and pointed hat, like that Aladdin wears in the cheap editions; a little varied by the Valentian in his party-colored mantle and his tow trousers, showing the bronzed leg from the knee to the blue-bordered sandals" (p. 20 - 21). Young Madrileños also excite Hay's pen: "Next comes a shouting band of the youth of Spain, strapping boys with bushy locks, crisp and black almost to blueness, and gay young girls with flexible forms and dark Arab eyes that shine with a phosphorescent light in the shadows" (p. 113). Titian's *Charles I* arrests Hay's eye too, with "his visor up over the eager, powerful face,—the eye and beak of an eagle, the jaw of a bull-dog, the face of a born ruler, a man of prey. And yet in the converging lines about his eyes, in the premature gray hair, in the nervous, irritable lips, you can see the promise of early decay, of an age that will be the spoil of superstition and bigotry" (p. 133).

The bullfight evokes Hay's most detailed depictions, with its masses of crowds, their movements, the ritualistic stages of the slaughter. Hay achieves a signal success when he describes the bull's first sight of the arena: "There is a bugle flourish, the door flies open, and the bull rushes out, blind with the staring light, furious with rage, trembling in every limb. This is the most intense moment of the day. . . . He stands for an instant recovering his senses. He has been shot suddenly out of the darkness into that dazzling light. He sees around him a sight such as he never confronted before,—a wall of living faces lit up by thousands of staring eyes" (pp. 81 - 82).

Although it is hard to choose examples from among the dozens that display Hay's rhetorical jibing, his targets are predictable. At the battle of St. Quentin, St. Lawrence was "the celestial officer of the day" (p. 213), says Hay, who also defines St. Leocadia as "her saintship" (p. 191). After the Portuguese had burned the Royal Alcázar of Toledo, Charles I "restored it just in time for the French to destroy it anew" (p. 209). Furthermore, the gilt tabernacle of Trezzo and Herrera at the Escorial "no longer exists," Hay tells us, because "it furnished a half-hour's amusement to the soldiers of France" (p. 219). Of Philip II, Hay writes: "One of the few luxuries this fierce bigot allowed himself was that of a new widowhood every few years" (pp. 219 - 20). One Velazquez portrait catches Philip IV "actually on his knees at his prayers!" (p. 133). It would seem that

Hay wants his satire both ways: a Catholic king who prays is a superstitious bigot, one who does not do so lays himself open to criticism.

Aristocrats and other favored beings fare no better with Hay than do Spanish saints and monarchs. The Count of Altamira receives a lavish subsidy from the government and in return "surrenders, while it is punctually paid, the privilege of hanging his neighbors" (p. 53). At one point Hay with doubly cutting pseudo-severity remarks that "it would . . . be unjust to the priesthood to consider them all as corrupt as royal chaplains" (p. 38). Not even a polyglot professor is spared: ". . . Alonso Sanchez [of the University of Alcalá de Henares] lectured in Arabic, Greek, and Chaldean, doubtless making a choice hash of the three . . ." (p. 287). With a straight face, Hay reports that "the law of the land imposed a heavy fine upon physicians who did not bring a priest on their second visit" (p. 43) to any given patient. Poor "Fa Presto" Giordano is ridiculed for his Escorial ceilings depicting "an army of martyrs . . . sailing with a fair wind into glory" (p. 221).

Ordinary citizens and their pleasures are also subjected to Hay's deft verbal attacks. Fickle bullfight spectators throw things at a timid matador; on one such occasion, "They threw orange-skins at him, and at last, their rage vanquishing their economy, they pelted him with oranges" (p. 84). Hay's eye is always peeled for attractive women, but it is not always rewarded: "I looked out and saw a group of brown and ragged women, each with an armful of baby" (p. 194). Dining with the rich politician Rivero may be fun—"What a culinary symphony his dinners are" (p. 318)—but too many soirées in Madrid feature what Hay calls "Tantalizing ices, crisped shades of baked nothing, arid sandwiches, and the feeblest of sugary punch" (p. 8).

Similes and metaphors in *Castilian Days* are numerous; and they are occasionally effective, often a bit bookish, and usually unelaborated. Most frequently they concern birds, animals, water, metals, sickness, light, and the classics. Thus, Velazquez sponsored Murillo "and watched with noble delight the first flights of the young eagle whose strong wing was so soon to cleave the empyrean" (p. 148). Cervantes's insulting little pension was "a bone thrown to an old hound, but he took it and gnawed it with a gratitude more generous than the gift" (p. 300). Hay describes a holiday parade and its horde of spectators as "a rivulet of procession meander[ing] . . . feebly through a wilderness of mob" (p. 100).

The typical dishonest Spanish politician has "a brow of bronze when detected and exposed in a misrepresentation" (p. 350). Impoverished Spain "is in a financial phthisis. It is not nourished by its revenues" (p. 399). The old days of credible miracles were for Hay "the twilight of belief" (p. 45), while the revolution of 1868 was once thought to augur "the fresh and dewy dawn of democracies" (pp. 369 - 70). Finally, Hay's tropes are somewhat too replete with Actaeons, Danaes, dryads, Menads, Narcissuses, Olympuses, and—in Toledo streets—even "daedalian windings" (p. 184).

Neoclassical also is Hay's employment of epithets, a few of which are memorable: thus we have "mitred infamy" (p. 38), Titian "the wonderful centenarian" (p. 150), Homer "the blind Scian" (p. 293), President John Tyler "this distinguished accident" (p. 351),[11] and a theater-ticket scalper "my shabby hidalgo" (p. 235).

Hay was almost a letter-perfect writer. But he does overuse "there" as an introductory function word, as in ". . . there is no class unrepresented. . . . There is nothing too precious to be parted with" (p. 77). He even dangles an occasional modifier, for example, the following: "Walking with my long-robed scholarly guide . . . , hearing him talk with enthusiasm of the glories of the past . . . , it was not difficult to imagine the scenes of the intense young life which filled these noble halls in that fresh day of aspiration and hope . . ." (pp. 289 - 90). A tiny grammatical error may be found by the alert in this line: "no one dreams of changing anything which their fathers thought proper" (p. 51). Hay could also write better than when he described Van Dyck's *Crowning with Thorns* as having "less dimensions" (p. 156)[12] than a comparable Rubens, or when he committed the double "that" in the following: "You may be reasonably sure that if you shut your door in the face of a Spaniard who is running for his life, that his hours are numbered" (p. 361). Out of parallel is this: "A Protestant cannot only live in Spain, but . . . he can die and be buried there" (p. 229). Finally, when Hay writes of a certain duelist that "there is probably no man in Paris less respected, unless we except his Imperial master" (p. 371), surely he means "if" rather than "unless." Such minor exceptions only prove that Hay followed virtually all the accepted rules of composition. America can boast of few more flawless literary technicians.

IV *Authorial Traits*

If Hay had chosen to publish his *Castilian Days* anonymously, as
he did his *Bread-Winners,* what kind of person might his readers
have judged him to be? First off, a loyal American Protestant, as has
been amply seen. A well-off idler too; for he seems to require no
employment, has abundant leisure and the means to travel comfortably, and evinces a certain hauteur. He is of a literary turn:
quotations from and paraphrases of British writers, especially
Shakespeare, are frequent. He chauvinistically mentions Walt
Whitman, Edgar Allan Poe, Ralph Waldo Emerson, Artemus Ward,
and Washington Irving. He knows Western art, roundly plumps for
his favorite artists, and ventures to disagree with standard travel-
book writers and art critics whenever he pleases.

Less immediately apparent here are traces of Anglo-Saxonism
long ingrained in Hay. He evinces sufficient sympathy for Jews who
were victims of Spanish oppression, but he displays no overt respect
for much that is Hebraic save commercial acumen. Moreover, we
notice his distinct, if muted, anti-Irish, anti-Celtic bias. When it
comes to Spain versus France, he is also anti-French. Still challenging analysis, he gradually begins to display a few other traits. He is
loyal to political party but indifferent to empty honor when it is
substituted for old-fashioned honesty. His great respect for
women—especially for their attractiveness, endurance, and maternal drive—has a touch of male chauvinism, particularly when he
hints that women are better off at home or in church, and not in the
political arena. He likes to generalize, as though he had more learning, experience, and *savoir faire* than could then have been the case.
Too frequently he attaches himself in dialogue and tableau to the
high-born, the brilliant, the distinguished; and seldom or never
does he stoop to chat—eye-to-eye—with a child, an actor, a servant,
a sacristan, or a beggar.[13]

All in all, *Castilian Days* is a remarkable, if biased, book of essays
about Spanish civilization. Although this work contains crisp observations about religious and political matters in Spain, and about her
art, history, scenery, and people, Hay also manages to tell us much
about himself. He generally writes so delightfully here that it seems
sad that this work was destined to be his only venture in the genre
of travel writing.

CHAPTER 6

Hay's Fiction

JOHN Hay wrote and published five short stories and a novel, and he dictated the plot of another story to his State Department friend Alvey A. Adee, who then wrote it and published it.[1] Hay's short stories are "Red, White, and Blue," 1861; "Shelby Cabell," 1866; "The Foster-Brothers," 1869; "Kane and Abel," 1871; and "The Blood Seedling," also 1871. His novel *The Bread-Winners* was serialized 1883 - 1884 and published in book form 1884. Hay never collected his stories for book publication, and he never officially acknowledged authorship of his novel.

In his fiction—as in his poetry, his travel essays, and indeed his other literary genres—Hay showed skill, imagination, genuine talent, and, ultimately, indifference. He simply refused to make a sustained commitment to a line of work which, had he chosen to follow it tenaciously, he would have mastered. His fiction is smooth, competent, and, in some respects, ahead of its time.

I Hay's Short Fiction

"Red, White, and Blue" is a thin piece of enlistment propaganda published soon after the start of the Civil War. The story opens in April, 1861, when Jerome Ryversant becomes engaged to Caroline Mayne, only to find his happiness threatened when he announces his intention to join his regiment. Because Caroline thinks that love should be stronger than patriotism, she weeps and bids Ryversant a chilly farewell. But she gradually becomes aware of the complexity of his honorable devotion; so, when he returns to her at the end of his three-month enlistment, she allows herself only a brief happiness and soon sends him back to duty and an undisclosed future. She explains, "As you would give up for its [the nation's] cause what is dearer than your own life, I give what is dearer than mine."[2]

Hay pleasantly sketches his two main settings: Caroline's sweet-

smelling boudoir and a hostess's flowery conservatory, in which the
proposal takes place. His characters are flat: Caroline is described
only in terms of fine clothes, pretty flowers, a pretty face, and
"feminine" lack-logic until she is humanized by contact with
Ryversant, who is all courtesy, rhetoric, patriotism, and stiff upper
lip. Curiously, Hay gives his heroine's brother Edgar Mayne a
background including French salons before he had himself experienced them. Male chauvinism is part of his male characters
here, if not of Hay; Edgar tells his sister, for example, "You are
pretty, Carrie; but such a doll!" She takes three hours to dress for
the waltz party; and, until the national emergency matures her,
"She . . . hated politics and newspapers!" Her room is filled with
"trifles"; and Hay finally blames it all on "her defective education
as a woman." Dialogue is romantically stilted: Ryversant wants to
keep Carrie's glove as "a guerdon of emprise." Hay includes a neat
little pattern of color symbolism: white glove with stain of red
orchis, "rose-Eden of Youth" (p. 666) and love, and hero's silken
cockade of red, white, and blue.[3]

In "Shelby Cabell," the narrator, an expatriate named Blair Harding, recounts his observations of a fellow Kentuckian in Paris.
Young Cabell, an engaging, unemployed ex-diplomat from the
Confederate side of the Civil War,[4] talks so colorfully of methods of
committing suicide that the narrator only tardily realizes that the
man is serious. When Cabell is rebuffed by the Marquise de
Bellechasse, an incomparably beautiful young American-born
widow, he makes everyone take note—the Parisian police, the
narrator, and even the horrified beauty—by splashily throwing
himself at her feet from the Arch of Triumph.

Paris is evoked well. Characterization is adept. The hero is
romantically disaffected, talks poetically, is generous to others as his
spare francs dwindle, eludes Keystone-Cop authorities, and topical-
ly refers to Sam Patch and his inspiring suicidal example. The
narrator anticipates several of Henry James's lucid reflectors—he is
cool, level-headed, and socially acceptable; but he is late and impo-
tent when aid is needed. The heroine also anticipates some of
James's, including his Madame de Mauves and the Princess
Casamassima, who, as Monteiro notes,[5] also drive frustrated lovers
to suicide. Jamesian as well is the heroine's father, an American
"Merchant Prince" named Brinton who, though antecedent to the
action, is memorably depicted as "a man enriched by sagacious
trade. . . . He was a square, grave, witty, shrewd, well-born
man . . . who could drive his own bargains and his own horses,

and buy his own books and his own wine, and who wouldn't be con-descended to by a prince. . . . A man whom no country on earth but America could send out. Every where else it requires one lifetime to make a fortune, and three to learn how to spend it."[6]

The main action, the suicidal plunge, is blatantly foreshadowed and is therefore less effective than several minor actions: a noctur-nal walk through Parisian streets, Cabell's brave exposure of a card cheat, the narrator's visit to the Marquise's petty court of admirers, a Twainesque incident in which a would-be suicide practices by let-ting an iron-mill trip-hammer smash not his head but his fist first—just a kind of rehearsal—and the narrator's ineffectual attempt to turn an arm of the French law loose on debtor Cabell to save him.

"The Foster-Brothers" is spotty but also intermittently strong and disturbing. The plot is complicated and improbable. Before the Civil War, Clarence Brydges, a handsome Southerner and the son of intractable proslavery Victor Brydges, pays a visit to his friend Cade Marshall (who reappears in Hay's "Kane and Abel" as an American legation secretary in Paris) of Moscow (i.e., Warsaw), Illinois. While there, Clarence meets spirited Mimi Des Ponts, who is Cade's casual friend. She lives with her widowed father Victor Des Ponts in Thebes, Missouri, which is situated across the flood-swollen Mississippi River. The two young people quickly fall in love; obtain permission from Mimi's "French creole"[7] father, a rich lawyer, to marry; and then write impatiently to Clarence's father to ask his blessing in case they cannot wait for his appearance at the ceremony. But the irascible Victor Brydges rushes from St. Louis to Moscow by a riverboat that suddenly bursts into flames just as Des Ponts, having made his will and his farewells, is out in his skiff for an airing. He rescues Brydges; then recognizes him as his own slave-owning master—and foster-brother—from whom he escaped to a splendid new life while the two were in France thirty years before. Des Ponts offers him honorable terms for his silence so that their children—now married—may remain happy. When he is selfishly refused, he turns murderous and suicidal, and descends to a watery death locked in an embrace with his adversary. Their bodies are washed ashore in this posture. Mimi and Clarence are misinformed to the effect that "from their graves your beloved fathers—one of whom lost his precious life in this noble effort to rescue the other from the waves—exhort you continually to love one another" (p. 544).

Such a bald summary almost makes a mockery of the operatic

84

plot, which, under the circumstances, is handled well because Hay
endows it with oneiric elements that are not necessarily related to
any attempt at total realism. Clarence has been sent by his father to
visit the North before the Abolition movement splits it from the
South. By chance a robbery report delays his boat at Moscow.
Visiting the flooded Missouri side of the river enables him to meet
Mimi, whose father is a figure of trouble and mystery. The lovers
ride horseback through sun-dappled woods along "the Carthage
road" (p. 540). A significant mix-up in the delivery of a telegram
obliges the honeymooners to miss old Brydges. Death by water
follows fire. Many of these incidents have inexplicable overtones.

The weird tale is vivified by several exemplary touches. The
rushing plot fails to disturb because of indisputable authorial control and the fresh, constantly surprising diction. Narrative summary
alternates with detailed scenes to create pleasant variety. The local
dialects are well imitated and include that of one lad with a combined Pike County and German accent. The muddy flood is as
brilliantly described as George Washington Cable might have
managed it. The significance of the title dawns on the reader long
after he has perhaps forgotten that it has nothing to do with
Clarence and Cade. The names Des Ponts (French, "of bridges")
and Brydges are only tardily linked, and old Brydges's first name is
cleverly delayed as well. There are several rather charming allusions
to Shakespeare. And the climax anticipates much in *Something of
Value*, Robert Ruark's memorable novel about "brothers" of
different colors. The parent-child theme is varied subtly. Imagery is
quite effective, especially when we read of Mimi and her father that
"Seeing them together you would think of a head in clay copied in
porcelain" (p. 539) and later that Des Ponts looks in the fire scene
like a Rembrandt. Racial intertwinings are modulated as skillfully as
they are in Albion W. Tourgée's *Royal Gentleman* or in Mark
Twain's *Pudd'nhead Wilson*. Mimi is marvelously frank and sen-
sual, like a Kate Chopin heroine. A town constable is amusingly
named Ketchum.

Monteiro provides some remarkable insights not only about "the
themes of slavery, miscegenation, and black versus white" but also
about another possibility: "Hay touches on an allegorical meaning
that perhaps he himself did not want: blotting out the facts of
heritage . . . will enable the young miscegenated couple to live out
their lives, hostage only to that fortune which is uniquely theirs."[8]

In "The Foster-Brothers," which has enough ingredients for a short novel, Hay offers an imperfect but profoundly disquieting parable that repays careful attention.

"The Blood Seedling" starts in the early 1840s when Tyler is president; is located near Chaney Creek, Illinois, close to Warsaw; and tells of jealousy, murder, and the inexorable revelation of evil. Allen Golyer (Hay used the last name in his ballad entitled "Golyer") inarticulately loves pert, buxom Susan Barringer, who might be swept off her rural feet by fancy traveling salesman Bertie Leon but for Golyer's secret interference. In fact, Golyer kills Bertie with a spade and buries him at the roots of an apple sapling which Colonel Blood (who appeared in Hay's ballad "The Mystery of Gilgal") has just let him transplant to start an orchard. With Bertie out of the picture, Susan says yes to Golyer, they wed and prosper, and twenty years pass in a flash. When the action resumes, a local, epileptic, pro-Swedenborg spiritualist named Gershom Chaney scribbles cryptic lines about a man with a spade during a well-attended séance one ghostly night. Golyer erupts with a confession, rushes into the night, and is found next morning near the roots of his luscious apple tree—dead by his own hand.

The story has wonderful possibilities but also its flaws. Monteiro rightly observes that its theme of "guilt that lies fallow and unexpiated" is Hawthornean; that Bertie "is typically dandified, philandering, and urbanely corrupt"; and especially that "the seedling . . . [is] a symbol for prosperity and goodness, laid out for his [Hay's] characters, before . . . [it] swell[s] into the reader's symbol for evil." But less convincing is Monteiro's assessment of "The Blood Seedling" as "Hay's finest story" or the critic's implication that it anticipates Hamlin Garland's "bleakly realistic stories of the agrarian 'west.' "[9] Hay's local-color details of dialect, place names, and rural descriptions are well handled; but his slightly supercilious narrator remains blind to any evidence of real Middle Western bleakness. A vitally important early flashback is awkwardly managed. The salesman's disappearance is never investigated, so far as the reader learns. The two central characters' domestic life is never dramatized, nor is Susan's view of it even seen. The medium is introduced late and too suddenly (somewhat as Madame de Bellechasse was in "Shelby Cabell"). And, finally, the titular symbol is allowed to stand forgotten too much of the time. Hay's "Blood Seedling" is a fascinating but abortive fictional effort.

"Kane and Abel," the last of Hay's short stories to be published, was probably written between the publication of "Shelby Cabell" and "The Foster-Brothers."[10] In it, Blair Harding, the narrator of "Shelby Cabell," introduces contrasting American twins—the dark, poetic, compassionate Kane Lennard, and the fair, intellectual, proud Abel Lennard—to the delights of Paris; and these include the beery dance hall, the Prado, where Kane meets and falls genuinely in love with a working girl named Marie Aucaigne. While his brother is at Trouville with their cousin, Madame de Bellechasse (who was introduced in "Shelby Cabell"), and her rich father, Lorthrop Brinton, Kane marries the girl and even innocently hires her former secret lover, a caricature of a Jew named Schnitzberg, as his valet. Learning by a letter from Kane about his marriage, Abel regards it—as would Brinton—as a disgrace to the family; and he therefore hurtles himself back to Paris, gets hold of some laudanum by improbable means, and poisons Kane to save their family honor. The grisette and her shabby "Schnitz" sneak out; but they are soon caught, and he—she is too lovely—is punished for murder.

Once again Hay gives us a flawed but absorbing piece of fiction. The plot is intricate, forced, and too baldly revealed. In a necessary flashback, we are told about the twins' doting, then lonely parents, but we never see them again. Through Kane's eyes, the bad heroine is captivatingly focused; but, as Monteiro observes, Schnitzberg is "grotesque, almost sub-human." Harding, once again like a Jamesian onlooker, remains uncommitted. This time Paris is insufficiently evoked by vague little lyric cries. Hay masks his literary clichés by having fair-haired, blue-eyed Abel kill swarthy but callow, unthinking, guiltless Kane. Although Monteiro considers the story "a sustained allegory of American innocence on trial before the courts of Europe,"[11] the narrative actually lacks both depth and finish.

As a short-story writer, Hay is always alert and interesting. He has an observant if cool eye, an ability to characterize deftly and to handle dialogue gracefully, and an inventiveness that enables him to give serious didactic turns to sensational material. He deplorably failed to continue to mine two rich American fictive veins he exposed from 1861 to 1871, before Tourgée, Twain, Howells, James, and Garland: the fate of bright, inexperienced Americans in glittering Europe; and the bittersweet lives of rural Middle Westerners near or along the Mississippi River, with troublesome racial problems thrown in.

II   *Hay's Novel*

Between his last story and his only novel, Hay married money, entered into a lucrative business arrangement in Cleveland with his conservative father-in-law, joined the right wing of the Ohio Republican party, did a brief stint of federal service in Washington, and traveled idly with his growing family. *The Bread-Winners* was written by a person made essentially different as a result of these experiences. Hay was not, however, an altogether different writer, although it may be valid to assert that he disguised his fictional style somewhat, so that readers of his signed tales could not blame him for *The Bread-Winners*.

The publishing history of this twenty-chapter novel is interesting. From August, 1883, through January, 1884, the *Century* ran six monthly installments of three or four chapters each; then Harper & Company issued the novel in book form in January, 1884, and reprinted it in 1893, 1899 (with an unsigned prefatory sketch by Hay), and 1916. Meanwhile, the New York *Times* serialized it on six Sundays in a row, starting July 30, 1905, less than a month after Hay had died. The 1916 Harper edition included a short introduction by Clarence Hay and also placed the author's name on the title page for the first time. In 1967, the first edition was reprinted by facsimile, and in 1973 the presumably "definitive" 1893 text was reprinted with a fine introduction and other front matter by Charles Vandersee.[12]

The Bread-Winners has been celebrated and criticized as America's first novel to oppose labor unions; but it was not the first. Thomas Bailey Aldrich's *Stillwater Tragedy* preceded it in 1880; and, as Hay rightly protested in his 1899 preface, "I have not discussed the labor problem at all."[13] "The Bread-Winners," so called, are not labor-union members but a small group of lazy malcontents and would-by anarchists from the working classes who take advantage of a general strike to try to loot some of the homes of the rich. Only about a third of the novel is devoted to Andrew Jackson Offitt, the leading "Bread-Winner," and his followers; and one of them is a smelly spiritualist medium who is so inept that anything he joins may be regarded as doomed. In only a couple of chapters does the strike figure centrally. The bulk of the novel concerns two tall, beautiful teenaged girls and the men they attract.

The Bread-Winners is set in Buffland, which is a portmanteau

place-name obviously derived from Buffalo and Cleveland; and the
town is located on a great lake near a rival lake town called Clair-
field (it is named Clevalo, also from Cleveland and Buffalo, in the
magazine version). The time of the action is the late spring and
summer of 187 - (1877, the year of the big railroad strike, in the
magazine version).[14] The principal character is Captain Arthur
Farnham, who, in his mid- or late thirties, is a Civil War veteran, a
childless widower, and the heir of much property from his grandfather. Mrs. Belding, aged fifty, is his well-to-do, next-door
neighbor on fashionable Algonquin Avenue, which is undoubtedly
based on Euclid Avenue, Cleveland. Her statuesque daughter is
Alice Belding, aged nineteen, who has just returned from a
finishing school in New York. Maud Matchin, a high-school
graduate of eighteen or nineteen, is the daughter of a hard-working
carpenter named Saul Matchin and his passive, religious wife. Sam
Sleeny, a vigorous, handsome young carpenter, works under Saul
and lives in the Matchin home. Andrew Jackson "Andy" Offitt—real name, Ananias Offitt[15]—is a greasy, ugly locksmith by
trade and a criminal by inclination.

Among the minor characters are Temple, the salty-talking vice-
president of a rolling-mill company and a stalwart friend of
Farnham[16]; Mayor Quinlin, who is pusillanimous, budget-
conscious, and Irish, and therefore suspect in Hay's eyes; and
Dalton, the adept but glib and effusive prosecuting attorney. And
there are others. Furrey is a foppish assistant bank cashier who likes
Alice. Jacob Metzger is a butcher and ward politician who discom-
fits Farnham. Leopold "Bolty" Grosshammer is a German gunsmith
and Farnham's "first freiwilliger" (German, "volunteer") (p. 191).
Nathan Kendall is a machinist from Maine—without accent,
curiously—and another of Farnham's militant friends. Euphrasia
"Phrasy" Dallas is an eligible debutante who does not interest
Farnham. Bowersox is a brutal, unemployed streetcar driver.
Farnham's sniffy British butler is Budsey, and his Scottish gardener
is Ferguson. Azalea Windom is an uppity high-school friend whose
attractions Maud eclipses in the fulness of time. Five still more
minor characters have names that are cleverer than they: Pen-
nybaker, a minor politician; Dr. Buchlieber, the near-sighted
librarian; Tony Smart, a city detective; Dr. Cutts, Farnham's physi-
cian; and Minnie Bell, Maud's little friend at the library.

In the complex, fast-paced plot, Captain Farnham, busy with his
rentals and other sources of income, his well-tended garden, and his

memories of life and wife in the West, is approached by gauche, brash, untrained, smolderingly attractive young Maud Matchin, who asks him to use his influence as president of the library board to obtain a minor clerkship in the library for her. After he promises to try, he visits Mrs. Belding and her suddenly mature and attractive daughter Alice next door. After Farnham is rebuffed at the library a few days later by a canny little coalition that favors a political appointment for the clerkship in question, he wrongly encourages Maud by telling her that he will try elsewhere for her and he even gives her a bouquet of flowers as luscious as she. Sam Sleeny, who is doing some carpentry for the rich captain, sees what transpires and tries to rebuke his girl Maud; but she roundly squelches him. He mutters darkly that he will have her if he dies for it. Thus the first, largely introductory magazine installment ends (chapters 1 - 4).

The next installment is unified around the theme of domination of one personality by another. Offitt is introduced, plies Sleeny with beer, inflames him with jokes about his failures with Maud—whom Offitt himself soon begins to covet—and persuades him to join the Brotherhood of Bread-Winners, a band of shirking workers who hate the rich. Next, Farnham compliments sullen Sleeny on his workmanship, reminisces before him about army buildings in the West, and amiably cows him. Relieved that Farnham likes his neighbor, Alice Belding, Sleeny takes Maud to a séance perpetrated by the local "mejum" Bott. When the blushing girl asks Bott for advice to the lovelorn, the idiot thinks he is her object and confuses her with a gush of mispronounced verbosity. Finally, Farnham invites the Belding women to his conservatory to watch his night-blooming *cereus grandiflorus* open almost sensually, and he behaves so poetically that Alice is smitten by him (chapters 5 - 8).

The next section is disunified. First, Maud, who decides to follow her spiritualist's advice, rushes to Farnham, tells him frankly that she loves him—Bott wanted her to tell Bott—is kissed roundly, but is then laughed at.[17] When Sleeny sees the kiss occur, he waves his hammer from the bushes. Even more improbably, Alice's mother also sees it and foolishly tells her daughter about the incident. When Farnham learns of a vacant position at the library, he gains the job for Maud as penance for his kiss. Feeling cocky, he then visits the Beldings and soon defines his love for Alice, but she rejects him and idiotically makes him promise not to bring up the subject again. (This action ends chapter 10 and marks the exact midpoint of the novel.) Oddly happy though rejected, Farnham goes riding through some riverside woods and encounters the Bread-Winners. One of them brandishes a pistol, while the others force Farnham to leave. He then attends a high-society party at the Temples' house, where he learns that there is to be a general strike, during which some Algonquin Avenue mansions are to be looted (chapters 9 - 11).

The ensuing installment is also choppy. The strike begins, and the mayor is so spineless that Farnham organizes his own deputized patrol. On Sunday, Maud tells her sullen, honest old father that she will not marry Sleeny; she verbosely rejects simpering Bott; and she finds herself reluctantly encouraging wily Offitt, who lies about his past and whom she asks to beat up Farnham. At night, while vagrants and ex-convicts stir up the strikers, a knot of Bread-Winners led by Offitt tries to attack the Belding and Farnham residences; but they are repulsed gorily by the captain's well-drilled troops. Alice thanks Farnham, but in too restrained and Victorian a fashion (chapters 12 - 14).

The penultimate installment starts the minute the previous one ends. That same night, Sleeny attacks Farnham with a hammer but is disarmed; the general strike soon dissolves; and peace is restored. Bott is jailed; Sleeny gets off lightly, with only a fine, but turns sullen all the same; and Offitt, who has escaped without detection, borrows Sleeny's new hammer. One night soon thereafter he would have crushed Farnham's skull and then filched his rent payments but for a timely scream: Mrs. Belding and Alice happened to see the would-be murderer, and the girl warned her captain so that all he suffered was a gashed head, a concussion, a fever, and the loss of his bank notes (chapters 15 - 17).

The last three chapters are exciting and melodramatic, and they conclude the plots involving the three leading men. Offitt, with the stolen money still in his pockets, informs against Sleeny, who is arrested. Then Offitt goes for Maud, whom he wants to join him on a voyage to Paris, or at least in bed on the way. But Sleeny escapes, rushes to the Matchin house, and rescues his now true love by throwing Offitt down and crushing his neck. Sleeny would have been convicted of murder but for the Belding women's testimony, and Maud's persuasive eloquence and lies. Sleeny and Maud thus start a strange marriage. Farnham, still feeling repulsed, tells Alice of his plans to go to Japan. But she says with perfect ambivalence, "It is the end of the world" (p. 275), sings to him, and they are soon in an understanding embrace (chapters 18 - 20).

Such a plot summary ignores substantive and stylistic virtues, but it exposes a few of the novel's weaknesses. Hay is careless in several respects. On occasion he awkwardly advances a particular action and then backs up to explain antecedent circumstances; for example, in chapter 9, he brings Maud to Farnham's home, has Sleeny watch the pair kiss, then explains that Mrs. Belding has also come calling and thus becomes another witness. In chapter 14, Farnham busily defends his property until he is informed that trouble is brewing at the Beldings' next-door place. Hay backs up again, employs a few more past perfects, and dramatizes Offitt's already issued threats to the irate widow—who, incidentally, is not terrified half enough under the circumstances. It is unquestionably difficult to trace two plot strands at once, but Hay is also awkward in following Offitt to Maud's place on the final fatal day and then in backing up to follow Sleeny there too.

The most incredible plot element is Mrs. Belding's tardy revelation to Alice that Farnham kissed Maud. Admittedly, the woman told the girl a chapter earlier that the good captain "is old enough to be your father" (p. 147), which is biologically but probably not sociologically true. Less reprehensible is Hay's careless habit of introducing a plot element and then not developing it. For example, Maud's married sister Jurildy Wixham appears early and, after a few later references, is dropped. Bowersox is badly wounded by Temple, is much later reported as worse, and then—silence. Whether Temple's horse won the race at Rochester—or even got there to compete—goes unmentioned. In general, the last half of the novel has a faster pace, is more melodramatic, and is critically less challenging.

Hay was rightly rebuked by contemporary readers for having adopted an aristocratic point of view.[18] We read that Andrew Jackson Offitt was named after the president because of "a servile worship of the most injurious personality in American history" (p. 123).[19] Metzger, the butcher politician, is reported as establishing a "corrupt rule" supported by a "floating crowd of publicans and sinners" (p. 101). As for frequenters of spiritualist "seeuns" (p. 131), "To people like the ordinary run of the believers in spiritism, the opera, the ballet, and the annual Zola are unknown, and they must take their excitements where they can find them" (p. 136). Carpenter Saul Matchin is tolerable because "he was of English blood, and had never seemed to imbibe into his veins the restless haste and hunger to rise which is the source of much that is good

and most that is evil in American life" (p. 75).[20] On the other hand,
when Sleeny accompanies Offitt to a meeting of the Bread-
Winners, the self-respecting laborer "was not particularly proud of
the company in which he found himself. The faces he recognized
were those of the laziest and most incapable workmen in the
town—men whose weekly wages were habitually docked for
drunkenness, late hours, and botchy work. As the room gradually
filled, it seemed like a roll-call of shirks" (p. 118).[21]

Closely related to Hay's narrative voice is his hero, Arthur
Farnham, who seems partially autobiographical because of his army
background, travel experience, bookishness, richly appointed home,
and occupation as custodian of wealth earned by others.[22] In subtler
ways, Hay tells his readers about himself without having to sign his
novel; for, ever critical of national legislators, he has Temple
describe some labor union orators as "fit for nothing but Congress"
(p. 226). Hay ridicules Buffland journalists for publishing in the
local *Bale-Fire* sensational and inaccurate accounts of Offitt's death.
A few pages later, he lampoons the American jury system.[23] He
never overlooks a chance to demean the Irish: Offitt writes for the
Irish Harp (p. 123); the most easily led and oratory-prone strikers
are Irish; and finally this sentence appears: "There was not an Irish
laborer in the city but knew his way to his ward club as well as to
mass" (p. 229). Why not?[24]

Hay must have felt secure in his anonymity—he even jokes about
it (p. 247)—for he makes Mrs. Belding's dead husband Jairus a
"famous bridge-builder . . . [who] left her with one daughter and a
large tin box full of good securities" (p. 90). Amasa Stone left his
widow, Hay's mother-in-law, two daughters and chests full of
securities. When Hay has Offitt castigate the rich of Buffland as
"vampires" (pp. 115, 123), the author was perhaps quietly thinking
of members of his Cleveland Vampire Club. He has such a fixation
on tall women that his big wife Clara, at least, must have felt complimented by some of the descriptions.

Contemporary readers criticized Hay's novel for its lack of
realism as well as for its hauteur. His reply included this dishonest
assertion: "I have little technical skill in writing." He also pleaded
that all of the coarse details involving striking laborers and their unwashed orators had come from "life-long observation" and also
from newspaper accounts (pp. 59 - 60).[25] Admirably realistic are
descriptions of Farnham's beautiful home,[26] the lush soirée at the
Temples' mansion, the mayoral and police offices and activities, the

alleys and cramped homes and shops of laborers, and even the lakeside sunsets whose mellow lights suffuse rich and poor with natural impartiality.

Yet, by objective standards, *The Bread-Winners* is not sufficiently realistic. For this reason, among others, it was subjected to a number of vicious, skillful parodies that include the following: "The Muffin-Getters" (*Life*, January 10, 1884); Henry Francis Keenan's *Money-Makers* (1884), which Hay tried desperately to suppress[27]; *The Other Side* (1886), by Martin Ambrose Foran; and Faith Templeton's *Drafted In* (1888), which continues the story of Farnham, Mrs. Belding, Alice, Maud, and Sleeny, but also adds some newcomers.[28] Although Hay may have thought he was being a realist, the age in which he wrote was still suffering from the lingering effects of effete romanticism. Without much doubt, the chapter that Hay's first readers liked best is the last one, in which Farnham and Alice gyrate in a conversational mating dance before he finally settles on her warm bosom.

It is possible to reconcile Hay's realistic purpose and some of his unrealistic techniques. In fact, David E. E. Sloane does just that by arguing that by caricature (Bott is repeatedly characterized by his facial spots), melodrama (Offitt's proposal to Maud is straight off the gaslit stage), and sentimentality (especially the dénouement), among other romantic devices, Hay actually underlines the realistic depiction of the contemporary social and political scene[29]—which he knew well and did not wish to see ruined.

It remains to note a few more excellences in this intriguing novel. Hay employs dialect so accurately that American lexicographers have cited him on many occasions.[30] For example, Maud wonders about Farnham thus: "Why should he put me down that way?" (p. 74). Later a petty politician whines at Farnham as follows: "You ain't on the make; you're fixed" (p. 164). Hay cleverly couples a concrete noun and then an abstract one, or vice versa, as when Sleeny appears full of "beer and wrath" (p. 117), or when labor agitators preach "with fervor and perspiration" (p. 224).[31] Alice and Maud are alike in so many ways, especially when they expose their beautiful forms before mirrors, as they like to do, that Alice's matrimonial success and Maud's probable marital misery may both be explained by reference to naturalistic causes. What but environment and chance are operating?[32] This was an area where Hay unwittingly began to tread and then quickly stepped back. He felt safer when commenting more generally about the battle of the sexes—females in the business world, how men can do women favors with propriety, the etiquette of proposal, the mystery of womanhood, and the like.

Altogether, then, Hay's *Bread-Winners* was a timely, popular, and controversial novel that still rewards the sympathetic reader. Unfortunately, its anonymous author chose neither to boast of his deed nor to follow it with more fiction that could have been concerned with diplomacy, foreign travel, journalism, politics, and high finance. Instead, John Hay ignored contemporary issues and turned back to Abraham Lincoln.

CHAPTER 7

Abraham Lincoln: A History

JOHN Hay began his collaboration with Nicolay on their *Abraham Lincoln: A History* before *The Bread-Winners* started to appear serially. In 1876, Hay wrote a little about Lincoln; the following summer, a little more; by the spring of 1879, enough for perhaps half a volume. Then came interruptions, including the composition of his novel, the final installment of which appeared in January, 1884. By then, Hay was back in stride with the steadier Nicolay; and, by late 1885, the two were able to promise the *Century* serial installments of *Lincoln*, which appeared from November, 1886, through February, 1890. The previous summer had been spoiled for Hay by proofs for the much longer book version, which was released in ten volumes from September through December, 1890.[1]

Nicolay and Hay drew upon their memories of and memoranda on Lincoln. They put to excellent use the countless relevant papers by Lincoln that they had been gathering for two decades. They absorbed information from the growing shelves of written material about Lincoln and from collateral reading. The two men collaborated at every stage, commented on each other's writings, and rewrote with such criticism in mind. Their preface makes it clear that the final result was, "in the fullest sense, and in every part, a joint work."[2] Dennett is probably correct in asserting that Nicolay contributed the techniques of the researcher and political historian and that Hay was "the biographer and the stylist." But it is untrue, as Paul M. Angle curiously alleges, that the combined style of the two is superior to that of either.[3] Clearly, Hay subdued his unique tone and mode to the exigencies of joint authorship, and he may also have improved the style of Nicolay, who was not an unusually gifted writer.

The result of their work is matchless; but, as Dennett suggests, their *Lincoln* is neither biography nor history. Lincoln too often dis-

appears from stage, particularly in the first chapters and during the
worst seasons of the Civil War. But of the five thousand books about
Abraham Lincoln,[4] perhaps the greatest American who ever lived,
the ten-volume effort of Nicolay and Hay is one of the most
valuable.

I Sources

To prepare for their biography and history, Nicolay and Hay consulted all available pertinent source materials, published and
otherwise; and they used for background *Appleton's Cyclopaedia of
American Biography*, the *Annual Cyclopaedia*, the *Congressional
Globe*, and several major newspapers, especially the New York
Tribune.[5] When they needed material of a more specific nature,
they consulted the work of experts as varied as Horace Binney (on
the writ of habeus corpus), Thomas Ford (on the history of Illinois),
George F. Tucker (on the Monroe Doctrine), various writers of
Opinions of the Attorneys-General, John Jay Knox (on United States
currency and notes), and Spencer Walpole (biographer of Lord John
Russell), and dozens of other specialists.

The most valuable material Nicolay and Hay present on Lincoln
comes from their own memoranda and from the previously unpublished papers of the martyred president. Since they remark at
one point that "it is not our custom to quote Mr. Lincoln's expressions from memory" (VI, p. 13; see also I, p. xiii), their written
notes are all the more precious. Nicolay's memoranda are especially
valuable, for example, when he and his co-author describe the formation of Lincoln's first cabinet (III, pp. 345, 352, 353, 370). To
Lincoln devotees, the value of Hay's diaries is incalculable; for,
without them, scholars would know less, for example, about Lincoln's attitude towards Generals George B. McClellan, Henry W.
Halleck, and John C. Frémont; about the shrewd timing of his
Emancipation Proclamation; about his handling of Missouri ex-
tremists; and about his thoughts concerning the Wade-Davis
Manifesto. Less valuable but wholly commendable is the authors'
use of previously published biographies and special studies of Lincoln by Ward H. Lemon, Josiah G. Holland, Isaac N. Arnold, A. T.
Rice, and a few others. William H. Herndon must have displeased
Nicolay and Hay as much as they annoyed him; for, early in their
work, they call him "a young, bright, and enthusiastic man" when

he first associated with Lincoln, but they soon add that he became "obstinately obtuse" (I, pp. 216, 273).

For material about the Civil War, Nicolay and Hay consulted the voluminous *War of the Rebellion: Official Records of the Union and Confederate Armies*, and various reports to and by the hard-working Congressional Committee on the Conduct of the War (II, p. 343; V, pp. 150 - 51).[6] They also read congressional session records, State Department and War Department archival materials, papers in the Confederate Archives, certain state legislative records, and essays published as *Southern Historical Society Papers*. Useful also were *Battles and Leaders of the Civil War*, Benson J. Lossing's *Civil War in America*, and Edward A. Pollard's *Lost Cause*. They also read other histories of the Civil War and the Confederacy, by authorities as far apart as Union General Andrew A. Humphreys ("the most thoroughly candid and impartial" [X, p. 166]) and rebel President Jefferson Davis, whose *Rise and Fall of the Confederate Government* the authors castigate (see III, pp. 199 - 201; X, pp. 256 - 76 *passim*).

Falling somewhere in between such sources are the autobiographies and memoirs of Union Generals Winfield Scott, Ulysses S. Grant, William T. Sherman,[7] Philip H. Sheridan, McClellan, Admiral David D. Porter, and Colonels Herman Haupt and Thomas Wentworth Higginson, among a score of others. Among the Confederate participants who reminisced were Generals Joseph E. Johnston, John B. Hood, and Jubal A. Early, and Admiral Raphael Semmes, as well as others. Specialized accounts such as Union General Manning F. Force's *From Fort Henry to Corinth* (an "admirable little book" [V, p. 326n]) and George E. Pond's *Shenandoah Valley in 1864*,[8] among dozens of others, proved helpful.

Much private manuscript material was consulted too, for example, Gideon Welles's "deadly diary" (V, p. 227n) and General Robert E. Lee's "Letter Book," both long since published. Mention should also be made of biographical material published some years after the Civil War but before Nicolay and Hay finished their work—material such as that of Frank H. Alfriend and Burton N. Harrison, who wrote separately about Davis; General Adam Badeau on Grant; Henry Cleveland on Confederate Vice President Alexander H. Stephens; John Esten Cooke and Confederate General A. L. Long, separately on Lee; Robert L. Dabney on General Thomas J. Stonewall Jackson (the authors quaintly call Dabney, in order,

Dr., Professor, General, and finally Major [V, pp. 394, 398, 404, 439]); Loyall Farragut on his father Admiral David Farragut; Francis W. Palfrey and W. C. Prime, separately on McClellan; and Jacob W. Schuckers and Robert B. Warden, separately on Lincoln's Secretary of the Treasury Salmon P. Chase.

The two historians are so confident about their thoroughness that they often—sometimes prematurely—remark that no records in certain fields exist, that records in other areas are meager, and that certain published accounts on various subjects are inaccurate or perhaps merely do not agree with majority opinions. They note, for example, that "we have no record of the specific reasoning of President Lincoln upon these points" or that "we have no further expression of Lincoln's views until the midsummer of 1862" (VI, pp. 123, 348); that "there are no authentic reports of the Confederate army for the days of battle [at Chickamauga]" (VIII, pp. 105 - 06); and even that "the constant policy of the Confederate authorities was to conceal their losses; there are even at this day no trustworthy estimates of them" (IX, p. 418). The authors undertake to correct Lincoln's early biographers, also the Comte de Paris, and even Grant's *Personal Memoirs* here and there (VIII, pp. 108, 250n, 386). Rarely do they express uncertainty as to the existence of a document; therefore, comments such as the following are unusual: "The full report of these occurrences [setting fires in fallen Richmond], written by General [Richard S.] Ewell, seems never to have been printed" (X, p. 206n). They deplore the loss of Lee's headquarters baggage near Amelia Court House, "with all its wealth of returns and reports" (X, p. 186).

In addition, Nicolay and Hay consulted more sources than all of those that have been indicated. A rare personal aside, appearing in the midst of their discussion of Lincoln on election night, November 8, 1864, describes "a great bundle of papers which lies before us as we write, filled with telegrams from every quarter annotated in his [Lincoln's] own neat handwriting, with a mass of figures which would have dismayed an ordinary accountant . . ." (IX, p. 383).[9] Such meticulous care with source material is characteristic of every chapter in the ten volumes, but Nicolay and Hay also select evidence from their mass of manuscript and published sources[10] to suit their fixed theses. In the process, they emerge as Protestant Christian defenders of Unionism, of Constitutional abolition, of the Republican party, and of a martyred president who was almost divine because of the comprehensiveness of his supernal intelligence and charitable heart.

II *Contents*

Abraham Lincoln: A History has 4,580 pages—perhaps 1,500,000 words—with scores of illustrations, many maps (mostly poor by modern standards), and a detailed index of more than 260 columns. Being both biography and history, it has the variety of an alternately close-up and panoramic scenario; for it concentrates first on Lincoln and then on his milieu. Paul Angle notes that in the second volume the method becomes apparent; the authors present one or more chapters of history with little or no mention of Lincoln, and then a chapter or two in which Lincoln is again the controlling subject.[11]

Volume I (1780 to May, 1856) is composed of five loose units. Chapters 1 - 4 concern Lincoln's family background, his father's difficult years in Indiana, the condition of Illinois in 1830, and Lincoln's childhood and early youth through 1831. Chapters 5 - 10 concentrate on Lincoln until his marriage: his part in the Black Hawk War (1832), his work as a surveyor and then as a state legislator (1834 - 1841), and his first residence in Springfield and his law practice there. Chapters 11 - 17 consider the duel Lincoln almost fought with James Shields; Lincoln's melancholy before his marriage (November, 1842); Lincoln in the United States Congress against a backdrop of the Mexican War (1847 - 1849), which he opposed; and then his escape back to Illinois and his circuit lawyer work there. Chapters 18 - 21, in a disunified manner, include essays on slavery in America, the repeal of the Missouri Compromise, and Lincoln's first encounters with Stephen A. Douglas. Finally, chapters 22 - 25 concern Kansas from 1854 to 1856—its Border Ruffians, the bogus laws that its illegal first legislators passed, the brave little Topeka Constitution, and civil war in the territory.

Volume II (May, 1856 to December, 1860) falls into five unbalanced parts. The first, chapters 1 - 6, starts where Volume I ended, in bloody Kansas, and proceeds through the presidential conventions of 1856, the near-fatal caning of Senator Charles Sumner by Congressman Preston S. Brooks in May, 1856, the history of the Dred Scott Decision of 1857, what both Lincoln and Douglas thought about it, and the proslavery Lecompton Constitution for Kansas. Chapters 7 - 10 detail Douglas's loss of national prestige, his fascinating debates with Lincoln, the Freeport Doctrine, and Lincoln's rise to national prominence through his nonsectional speeches in Ohio (October, 1859). Chapter 11 is a separate unit about John Brown. Chapters 12 - 16 move from Lincoln's Cooper

Institute Speech (February, 1860) to the Charleston and Baltimore
conventions that split the Democratic party, to the Chicago convention that named Lincoln as the Republican party standard-bearer,
and to his election in November, 1860. Chapters 17 - 29 comprise a
painful section that details the ineffectuality of President James
Buchanan and his noncoercion, concession policy; the treason
within his own cabinet; the momentum of secession conventions
and declarations; the seeming impotence of Congress; and the
vulnerability of Union forts at Charleston, South Carolina.

Volume III (December, 1860, to April, 1861) is an ill-organized
combination of three parts of unequal length, the first and third of
which are additionally disunified by biographical and historical
digressions. Chapters 1 - 15 contrast the conniving of Secessionists
and the defensiveness of those in power around Buchanan.
Chapters 1 - 5 mostly detail the efforts of South Carolina to take
Fort Sumter without bloodshed; chapter 2, however, is a digressive
essay on the personal liberty bills by means of which several
Northern states sought to frustrate the hunters of fugitive slaves.
Chapters 6 - 11 describe the temporary strengthening of Buchanan's cabinet by the replacement of traitorous John B. Floyd as
secretary of war with Joseph P. Holt, the replacement of old Lewis
Cass as secretary of state with Jeremiah S. Black (whose functions as
attorney general were taken over by Edwin M. Stanton), and the
replacement of Secessionist Philip F. Thomas (who had replaced
disloyal Howell Cobb) as secretary of the treasury with John A. Dix;
the failure of the *Star of the West* to run the rebel blockade of
Charleston harbor; and the Sumter stalemate and the "truce" at
Fort Pickens in Florida. Chapters 12 - 15 place bold Secessionist
maneuvers against compromise and amendment failures. Chapters
16 - 18 concentrate on Lincoln again and present the reasons for his
refusal to be drawn into preinauguration discussions. The last of the
three parts (chapters 19 - 26) totals eight chapters, of which five
concern Lincoln. Chapters 19 - 22 describe his heartbreaking
farewell to Springfield; the foiling of an apparent assassination plot
in Baltimore; the March 4 inauguration ceremony, including the
address text together with annotated drafts; and the formation of
Lincoln's seven-man cabinet. The next chapters (23 - 25) take up
his gradually evolved strategy for meeting rebel threats at Sumter
and Pensacola, and in the confused state of Virginia. The final
chapter 26 characterizes Lincoln on the eve of war.

Volume IV (April to November, 1861), which is concerned only

with the events of the first seven months of the Civil War, is a
dramatic twenty-five chapter unit of four parts. Chapters 1 - 8 tell
of the successful uprising in defense of Unionism and of the initial
dangers besetting Washington, D.C., because of its isolated position
near unstable Maryland. Chapters 9 - 12 report the Secessionist
successes in Texas, the failure along the border of the Department
of the Ohio (organized under McClellan), the qualified success in
troubled Missouri, and the early failures in loyal Kentucky.
Chapters 13 - 15 set in perspective the quick coups (sometimes
against the popular will) of the Confederate military league, composed of a hard core of seven slave states (South Carolina, Mississippi, Florida, Alabama, Georgia, Louisiana, and Texas) and four less
insurgent interior slave states (Virginia, Arkansas, Tennessee, and
North Carolina); the rallying of Unionist Northern states (plus the
border states of Delaware, Maryland, Kentucky, and Missouri); and
English and French duplicity in half-recognizing the Confederacy.
Chapters 16 - 25, which form a sprawling block, begin and end with
considerations of McClellan from the time he took leisurely command in Ohio until he replaced retiring old Scott as Union general-
in-chief. Here Nicolay and Hay dramatically contrast Grant to
flashy, inept McClellan; they praise Scott's disregarded Anaconda
plan to encircle the rebellious South; they discuss the loyalty of
Western Virginia and of Congress; they detail Northern military
failures, culminating in First Bull Run (First Manassas) and then
Ball's Bluff; they expose problems with Southern blacks; and they
criticize the grandstanding of Frémont as well as of McClellan.
Throughout, Lincoln is depicted as patient, tactful, tolerant, and
sagacious.

The first five parts of Volume V (May, 1861, to August, 1862)
chronologically overlap the previous volume; then the history of the
Civil War is carried well into its second year. The whole volume,
which has three distinct parts, is therefore not a unit separate from
the previous volume but rather an integral part of and then an ex-
tension of it. In chapters 1 - 7, the authors begin by retrogressing to
the Union naval buildup, climaxing with successes at Cape Hatteras
and Port Royal; they then recite the Trent Affair; and they discuss
the military stand-off in Tennessee and the sluggishness of most
Union generals in the West except Grant and George H. Thomas.
Chapters 8 - 17 are a jumpy sequence that begins with Lincoln's
replacement of Simon Cameron as secretary of war by energetic
Stanton; details Union strategic plans around December, 1861;

recounts the rebel evacuation of Manassas; shows McClellan's ineptness in the Chesapeake area; relates Grant's capture of Forts
Henry and Donelson; delineates Lincoln's plan for "compensated
abolishment" to end slavery; and portrays the continued Union
naval successes, off North Carolina, and up and down the Mississippi River, especially around New Orleans.[12] Chapters 18 - 24 report
the unwillingness of Union armies to follow up stalemates and tac-
tical successes with anything resembling strategic victories (Grant at
Shiloh [Pittsburg Landing], Halleck at Corinth, and especially
McClellan, first at Yorktown, then at Seven Pines, finally during the
Seven Days). A fine if partisan feature of chapters 21 - 23 is the
adverse criticism of Jackson and Lee, while chapters 20 - 24
denigrate McClellan and nearly canonize Lincoln.

Volume VI (August, 1862, to January, 1863, with terminal
chapters adducing evidence from beyond that limit) opens with a
chapter that belongs at the end of Volume V since it concerns Union
General John Pope and Second Bull Run (Manassas). The remain-
ing twenty chapters fall into six parts only loosely connected.
Chapters 2 - 4 focus on international power plays involving Mexico,
England, France, and both belligerents of the Civil War. Chapters
5, 6, and 8 concern the prickly problem of emancipation of black
slaves. Chapters 7, 9, and 10 report the Union horrors at Antietam
(Sharpsburg), McClellan's subsequent removal, and the Fredericksburg débacle of General Ambrose E. Burnside, who was
McClellan's reluctant replacement. Chapters 11 and 12 discuss the
fiscal policies of Chase, Lincoln's secretary of the treasury, and the
cabinet crisis that Chase's personal duplicity provoked. Chapter 13
is devoted to Union General Don Carlos Buell's success at Perryville
and Union General William T. Rosecrans's occupation of Mur-
freesboro. Chapters 14 - 21 straggle through subjects essential to
Abraham Lincoln: A History, but the material could have been
placed almost anywhere, certainly a little earlier or somewhat later:
the admission of West Virginia to statehood; Lincoln and the
churches; military governors—especially in Tennessee, North
Carolina, and Louisiana—and instability in Missouri; and Lincoln's
continuing problems with respect to blacks—abortive colonization,
the Emancipation Proclamation, and Negro Union soldiers and
Confederate retaliation thereto. It is easy to criticize the organization of this catch-all volume, but it would be difficult to reorganize
its diverse materials any better.

Volume VII (July, 1862, to October, 1863, with evidence to be dated later concerning Charleston, Andersonville, and Mexico) contains sixteen chapters, which fall into four unequal parts. Chapters 1 and 2 concern the Union draft and the New York draft riots of July, 1863. Chapters 3 and 4 describe the blockade of Charleston and other rebel ports, and General Joseph Hooker's gory débacle at Chancellorsville. Then comes a stirring unit—chapters 5 - 11—in which Grant's doggedness, ending with the fall of Vicksburg and Port Hudson (chapters 5 - 7, 10, and 11), is counterpoised against Lee's invasion of Pennsylvania, his defeat by General George G. Meade at Gettysburg, and Lee's escape back toward Richmond (chapters 8 and 9). The last part of the volume (chapters 12 - 16) is disunified but vital: it recounts the story of turncoat Clement L. Vallandigham; the peace-party machinations during various 1863 elections; the short-lived reign of Maximilian, Emperor of Mexico[13]; the fall of Forts Sumter and Wagner; and the ghastly story of prisoners of war. This volume is the most absorbing of the entire series.

Volume VIII (February, 1863, to June, 1864, with essay chapters ranging before and later) has twenty chapters, which fall into five parts. Chapters 1 and 2 concern conspiracies of Secession sympathizers in the North—some silly, many gory—and the inevitable suspension of the privilege of the writ of habeus corpus. Chapters 3 - 6 detail campaigns in Tennessee—at Chickamauga, Chattanooga, and Nashville. The next six chapters (chapters 7 - 12) form a grab-bag unit that deals with Lincoln's Gettysburg Address, his annoyance with Missouri radicals and conservatives, Meade's inconclusive maneuvers along the Rapidan River, rebel efforts in England and France to obtain ironclads and diplomatic recognition in 1863, Union military forays into Florida and Louisiana, and Senator Samuel C. Pomeroy's circular supporting Chase's foolish effort to take Republican party control from Lincoln. Chapters 13 - 15 are devoted to Grant, who was named general-in-chief in March, 1864, and who promptly tested Lee's strength in the wilderness and elsewhere—almost suicidally. The volume ends with a drum call of five quick chapters (chapters 16 - 20) that detail the political and military maneuvers that brought freedom to Arkansas, Louisiana, Tennessee, Maryland, and Missouri.

Volume IX (May, 1864, to March, 1865, with many essay extensions), in twenty chapters, reveals little unity except that which a generally chronological forward movement provides and except for the fact that it begins with Sherman about to leave Chattanooga and ends with his capture of Savannah. The chapters falls into nine parts. Chapter 1 discusses Sherman's pressure on Johnston from Dalton to the Chattahoochee River. Politics are the next subject (chapters 2 - 5): the convention that splinter Republicans held in Cleveland to nominate Frémont for president in May, 1864; Lincoln's June renomination at Baltimore; disaffected Chase's resignation and replacement; and Lincoln's veto of the Wade-Mason Bill, which proposed radical reconstruction measures. Chapters 6 and 10 describe the end of the rebel navy. Chapter 7 concerns Early's attack on Washington. Chapters 8 and 9 discuss abortive, unofficial peace missions. Chapter 11 narrates the Democratic party nomination of McClellan for president in what the partisan authors label "The Chicago Surrender." A military unit follows, in dramatic contrast (chapters 12 - 14): Hood's evacuation of Atlanta and Sheridan's successes at Winchester and elsewhere soon thereafter. Then comes a political unit (chapters 15 - 17) that deals with the changes Lincoln made in his cabinet in late 1864 and early 1865, his reëlection, and his magnanimous nomination of shifty Chase to become chief justice of the Supreme Court. In the final section (chapters 18 - 20) a discussion of reconstruction philosophies is sandwiched between descriptions of the siege of Petersburg, Virginia, and Sherman's march through Georgia. A notable feature of this penultimate volume is the skill with which topic after topic is thoroughly and finally treated, though in violation of chronological order, so that Lincoln's story can proceed, in the last volume, to its destined tragic end with a minimum of interruption.

Volume X (October 1864 to the end) contains eighteen chapters and the index to all ten volumes. The chapters may be divided into six parts. Chapters 1 - 3 deal with Union victories at Franklin, Nashville, Fort Fisher, and Wilmington, and over the Confederate ironclad the *Albemarle*. The next four chapters (chapters 4 - 7) are political ones that discuss the Thirteenth Amendment; an unsanctioned project to entice the Confederates to make peace with the Union and then join forces with it to conquer Mexico; Lincoln's conference with Stephens at Hampton Roads; and Lincoln's second inauguration. Chapters 8 - 13 detail Union victories: Grant over Lee at Five Forks, Lee's surrender at Appomattox, the fall and occupation of Richmond, Johnston's surrender to Sherman, and the capture of Davis. Chapters 14 - 16 describe the assassination of Lincoln, the fate of the conspirators, and Lincoln's funeral cortege and burial. Chapter 17, which discusses the surrender of hold-out rebel units in Alabama and Texas, provides casualty figures and summarizes the material costs of the war. Chapter 18 is a magnificent essay about Abraham Lincoln's immortal fame.

A work of this magnitude must have been extremely difficult to organize. It moves generally in chronological order, as this summary of its volumes suggests. A notable feature is its overall balance. Of some interest may be the following statistics, which are indicative of relative substantive stresses. Events mainly European are treated in seven chapters; American pre - Civil War political activities (largely relating to slavery), fifty-five chapters; American political activities during the Civil War, forty-seven; military and naval engagements, and allied considerations, seventy-four; material mostly concerning Lincoln before he became president, twenty-four; and material on Lincoln as president and commander-in-chief, seventeen. Naturally, many, if not most, of the 224 chapters fall into more than one category each.

III   *Schisms Everywhere*

Nicolay and Hay repeatedly show that people on both sides of the titanic Civil War invoked God's support, for each side believed in the righteousness of its cause. Apt therefore are the following lines from Herman Melville's impartial war poem "On the Slain Collegians":

> Each went forth with blessings given
> By priests and mothers in the name of Heaven;
>   And honor in both was chief.
> Warred one for Right, and one for Wrong?
> So be it; but they both were young—
> Each grape to his cluster clung,
> All their elegies are sung.

In his private thoughts, Lincoln extended this theological position. In September, 1862, while pondering the relationship of the government to God, he privately wrote thus: "The will of God prevails. In great contests each party claims to act in accordance with the will of God. Both *may* be and one *must* be wrong. God cannot be *for* and *against* the same thing at the same time. In the present civil war it is quite possible that God's purpose is something different from the purpose of either party . . . [H]e could give the final victory to either side any day. Yet the contest proceeds" (VI, p. 342).[14]

Human forces beyond the American borders also joined the contest. England and France may have been publicly neutral, but their various spokesmen—especially before Gettysburg and Vicksburg enlightened them—hoped in private for a Confederate victory which would necessarily weaken American potency in the New World, shatter the Monroe Doctrine, and permit European military and then politico-commercial adventures abroad. In addition, Canada harbored Secessionist conspirators and even bank robbers. France hoped that the cause of the American rebellion might promote imperialism, French style, in Mexico.

During the Civil War, political factionalism prospered in the democratic North more easily than it could under Davis's "imperious military dictatorship" (III, p. 397; see also IV, p. 265) in the South. War for Unionism against slavery was never universally popular in the North, as the history of the border states and of the draft riots attests. Lincoln was in imperfect control of his own Republican party, had to contend with radicals and conservatives who thought that he was proceeding either too slowly or too rapidly, and was constantly harassed by Democratic party members of various political and military persuasions. Irresponsible peace missions were another source of embarrassment to him. When McClellan ran against Lincoln for president in 1864, the general received eighteen votes for every twenty-three cast for Lincoln.[15]

Each of the country's rival war cabinets also offers proof of ineradicable divisiveness. In Lincoln's, William H. Seward (State), Stanton (War), and Welles (Navy) are the most highly praised; but Chase's fiscal wizardry, though not his self-delusion, is also commended. Almost all other members of his cabinet caused Lincoln pain at one time or another. Curiously, of Davis's overshadowed political subordinates, only Stephens is accorded even partial praise; but he—like Europe, America, its political parties, and most of the leaders not only political but also military on both sides—was self-divided, at times almost to the point of schizophrenia. Of the Confederate vice president, the authors write: "Mr. Stephens was a very incarnation of political paradoxes. Perhaps in all the South there was not another man whose personal desires were so moderate and correct, and whose political theories were so radical and wrong" (X, p. 128).

Both military establishments were deeply troubled. The Union army suffered, especially before Chickamauga and Chattanooga, under wretched, disaffected, even disloyal leadership. McClellen, Frémont, and to a lesser extent Burnside, Buell, Halleck, and even Meade, among others, are criticized in varying degrees. On the other hand, Union naval commanders, especially Admirals Farragut, Porter, and John A. Dahlgren, and certain junior officers of unusual daring and luck—for example, Commander William B. Cushing—deserve unqualified praise and receive it. Lee was a military genius if also—according to the partisan strictures of Nicolay and Hay—a hypocrite, deserter, and traitor, if consideration is given to his behavior and comments late in April, 1861 (IV, pp. 98 - 102, 158 - 59). The authors also point out defects in his tactics if not his strategy; but they readily admit that, like Lincoln, he deserved to become something of a legend—in Lee's case, for his storied invincibility. Most of Lee's generals receive merited praise, with the exception of Pierre G. T. Beauregard, Braxton Bragg, Hood, Jackson, and Nathan Bedford Forrest. Rebel naval activities are generally deprecated, especially those of murderous privateers such as Semmes. Generals receiving the most praise are, for the Union, Grant, Sheridan, Sherman, Thomas, and James B. McPherson; for the Confederacy, James Longstreet, Johnston, E. Kirby Smith, and William J. Hardee, in addition to Lee.

Lincoln too, towering at the center of this massive study, was a formidable congeries of traits; and his life was a sequence of improbable, compelling experiences. His story is lovingly told; his decisions, reverently explained; his granitic character, idolized; and his example, which he self-effacingly, perhaps in truth unconsciously, offered to his unitary nation and to the world, no less than apotheosized. Most frequently demonstrated in this long biography are Lincoln's patience, intelligence, essential nobility, self-reliance, personal integrity, indifference to self, forebearance, magnanimity, tact, kindness, firmness, and abiding hope. In one of their few really fresh similes, Nicolay and Hay compare Lincoln's patience to "that of nature, which in its vast and fruitful activity knows neither haste nor rest" (X, p. 355—see also IV, p. 151; IX, p. 77; X, p. 132).

IV "*War and Politics*"

"War and Politics, campaign and statecraft, are Siamese twins, inseparable and interdependent; and to talk of military operations without the direction and interference of an administration is as absurd as to plan a campaign without recruits, pay, or rations" (IV, p. 36).[16] This statement expresses a controlling thesis of paramount importance in *Lincoln* by Nicolay and Hay.

The significance of an American leader in wartime must be defined in terms not only of his political canniness but also of his military sophistication. During the Civil War, many influential persons were adept politically or militarily, but few were experts in both realms. Lincoln, however, was a political and military genius.[17] Hooker merited Lincoln's moderate words of praise: "I . . . believe you do not mix politics with your profession, in which you are right" (VII, p. 87). But Lincoln had to mix war and politics. South of the border, Bragg was right militarily, but he erred in his political reasoning (VI, p. 275). On the other hand, negligent Burnside, against whom Meade, with Grant's concurrence, preferred charges after Petersburg, was improperly exonerated by the Committee on the Conduct of the War because his "political orthodoxy . . . outweighed in their minds the purely military judgment of Grant and Meade" (IX, p. 426). John A. McClernand may have been a splendid politician; but, unlike his friend and fellow Illinois Democrat, General John A. Logan, he displayed no accompanying "aptitude for military command" (VII, p. 136); and, though he became a general, he was ultimately so ineffective that Grant removed him. Rare was an able soldier also perspicacious politically. For example, Rosecrans failed to see the adverse political consequences of his military sluggishness during his march to Chattanooga and, once there, tried Lincoln's almost limitless patience by wiring the War Office several cloudy political insights (VIII, pp. 67, 114). On the other hand, Sherman may have distrusted Union headquarters—"He regarded Washington with whimsical horror as a sink of corruption and iniquity, and thought that no good could come out of it"—but he brilliantly recognized the subtle political as well as the obvious military implications of his March to the Sea (IX, pp. 276, 477). Although Grant often saw military movements in terms of political consequences, Republicans Nicolay and Hay seem too generous when they praise Grant's tactically rash, early movement south of Vicksburg in March, 1863: ". . . it is altogether probable that what are contemptuously called by military writers political considerations, which Grant was too wise a man to disregard, had much to do with this final choice" (VII, p. 156).

Until Lincoln found his general in Grant, even he made mistakes because fate would not let him base his decisions on politico-military reasons. After Second Bull Run, Lincoln made unsoldierly McClellan commanding general of all the troops defending Washington; and the president did so against cabinet advice for excellent political reasons (VI, pp. 21 - 29). More effective militarily was Lincoln's Emancipation Proclamation, because his reasoning was neither political alone nor military alone, but together (VI, p. 108 - 10, 148, 167; IX, pp. 106 - 108). One of the finest features of this biography is the manner in which it persuades the reader gradually that Lincoln's skill in fusing military and political considerations became awesome. His biographers write, for example, that, after McClellan's failure before Richmond, "The necessity of a comprehensive rearrangement of military affairs was upon him [Lincoln], and it was but natural that it should involve a revision of political policy." As a result, he decided to issue the Proclamation, which would both stir public political opinion and tip the military scales: "He recognized . . . that in a republic the talisman which wrought the wonders of statesmanship and the changes of national destiny was public opinion." The authors then carefully conclude: "We now know that in the use of this talisman he was the most consummate master whose skill history has recorded" (VI, p. 120).

Southerners in support of continued rebellion are described as praying to their God for a combination of fortuitous circumstances, which, when defined, illustrate most succinctly the Siamese-twin relationship of politics and the military: ". . . the two [political] parties in the North in 1864 were differentiated with sufficient definiteness in the public mind as the peace and the war parties. In the South there was no shade of doubt as to this distinction. The hopes and prayers of the revolt were centered on McClellan's success [in the presidential election]. They deplored Confederate military disasters more for their political effect in the North than for any other reason" (IX, p. 352). In a stunning rhetorical stroke, Nicolay and Hay even suggest that voting is comparable to fighting: ". . . with the picket firing in Vermont and Maine [state elections] in September [1864], . . . the grand guard fighting in October [elections], in the great States of Pennsylvania, Ohio, and Indiana, and the final battle all along the line . . . in November" (IX, p. 369). Elsewhere, the authors write of Lincoln's successful employment of the bullet and the ballot, and point out that his reëlection simplified both political conditions and military prospects (VII, p. 363; X, p. 91).

V   *"The Steady Pace . . . of . . . Fate"*

"The armies of the Union were closing in from every point of the compass. Grant . . . Thomas . . . Sheridan . . . Sherman . . . were moving . . . with the steady pace and irresistible progress of a tragic fate" (X, p. 156). So Nicolay and Hay describe the beginning of what proved to be Lee's crushing defeat at Five Forks. But in reality the pace resounds through every volume of the whole work. Sometimes events seem merely lucky or accidental. At Chickamauga, Thomas happened while going through "an open bit of woods" to spy "a body of rebel infantry" and soon turned chance into "several hundred prisoners" (VIII, p. 104). During the Wilderness, Lee is depicted, perhaps erroneously, as deluded into issuing Early some bad orders: "Yet—so strange are the chances of war—this flagrant error inured to Lee's advantage. He . . . succeeded, favored by his own mistake and a fortunate disobedience of orders in his lieutenant . . ." (VIII, p. 369). Often, especially during the first years of the war, fate seemed to be resolutely against the Union cause. At First Bull Run, "Fate [was responsible] for the panic" (IV, p. 360), we read. During Shiloh, "Doubtless Halleck felt that the Fates were against him" (V, p. 309). And at Antietam, "Fortune, weary of having her favors rejected by General McClellan, . . . turned to the other side . . ." (VI, p. 141). Sometimes fate played cruel jokes, as when Confederate General Micah Jenkins was accidentally killed by his own men, "by . . . curious fatality" (VIII, p. 366) just a year after Jackson had suffered an identical fate in the same woods. Momentous Gettysburg evokes more phrases like "the hand of Providence," "destined to the terrors and the honors," "the ordainment of events," and "the same inevitable decision" (VII, pp. 234, 236, 245, 258) than any other event in the entire history.

At times, such comments have a naturalistic coloration, as when the authors opine that "the vices and virtues of the [Western] pioneers were such as proceeded from their environment" (I, p. 16), or when they explain that French politics in Mexico "faded away in logical and predestined disappointment and discredit" (VI, p. 34). But men ask for trouble when they deliberately let fate's dice make their decisions for them, as when Burnside irresponsibly selected by lot the least able of three possible divisional commanders to lead a bloody charge at Petersburg (IX, p. 421). The worst leaders hold fate responsible for all their deeds. In the authors' view, such a one was John Brown: "Perverted Calvinistic philosophy is the key which unlocks the mystery of Brown's life and deeds" (II, p. 209), they too airily asseverate. On the other hand, the most eminent leaders are those favored by merit as well as fate: "The success and fame of generals is the joint result of merit and of opportunity; and Grant was, beyond all comparison, the most fortunate of American soldiers" (VIII, p. 336). After the war, when the country was divided into nineteen military departments, the generals named to head them formed "a roll of the men . . . most favored by fortune and their own merits" (X, p. 338).

Many expressions of fatalism here are mainly poetic, but some are quite moving all the same. Thus, as July 4, 1863, approached, "It seemed as if the stars in their courses were fighting to make everything . . . gild with new luster the anniversary of American independence," while the range of hills around Gettysburg "was a cyclopean fortress, framed for its purpose before the birth of man" (VII, pp. 322 - 23, 237). More momentous are the several suggestions that Lincoln was marked by destiny. In 1849, he not only failed to become commissioner of the General Land Office but also declined the governorship of Oregon. Returning to Illinois instead, "he went about his work there until his time should come" (I, p. 297). When it came in 1860 and then came again upon his renomination in 1864, everything conspired against his Democratic party opponents; in fact, "the stars in their courses seemed to fight against them" (IX, p. 351). The authors wonder earlier what would have happened if in 1856 Lincoln had run for vice president—with "powerless gavel"—on the Republican party ticket that starred "impulsive Frémont"; then they add, "But the hour of destiny had not yet struck" (II, p. 36).

"If"—together with its substantively identical but syntactically varied form beginning "Had . . . "—is frequently used here. Sometimes Nicolay and Hay bluntly ask "What if . . . ?" What if Frémont had run in 1856? More often, however, the authors bleakly answer "what if" questions. If President Buchanan had acted vigorously, there might have been no Civil War. Had Scott's Anaconda been adopted, the war might have been shortened. If between Fort Donelson and Shiloh one Union general had been appointed to command all troops west of the Alleghenies . . . If Generals Frémont, Nathaniel P. Banks, and Rufus Saxton had pursued Jackson, in May 1862, as Lincoln had urged . . . And so on and on. The authors' treatment of Antietam rings with pathetic

"ifs" (VI, pp. 136n, 137, 138). Then if Hooker, at Chancellorsville
. . . If Meade could have forced Lee to join battle at Pipe Creek instead of at Gettysburg . . . If Sheridan had followed Early faster
after Fisher's Hill . . . The account of Petersburg also abounds in
"ifs," including a sentence that must have cost widowed and
orphaned readers of the time much agony: "An hour more of
daylight might have hastened the capture of Richmond by six
months" (IX, p. 409).

But, as Lincoln said, "the contest proceed[ed]" through four fatal
years. If we could change aspects of our fate, all of us would. Then,
however, as everyone knows, fate would not then be fate—under
such circumstances.[18]

VI *"This Saving Grace"*

Historical as well as other written works that describe political
and military events in a context featuring such words as "fate,"
"fortune," "destiny," and "if" are likely to have a darkly humorous
tonal accompaniment, if only because what people hope for and
what chance grants them are usually so very different. *Lincoln* by
Nicolay and Hay is no exception. At one point they describe Chase's
inveterate habit of protesting his loyalty and then taking umbrage
at Lincoln's superior intelligence and tact. After detailing an incident involving Chase's conceit, the historians close thus: "Any
statesman possessing a sense of humor would have hesitated; but, as
we have said, Mr. Chase was deficient in this saving grace . . ."
(IX, pp. 90 - 91).[19] Given their subject, the historians' humor is
perhaps fated to take ironic, sarcastic, and grim turns rather than
graceful ones, most of the time.

The finest glints of really pleasant humor in the whole work
radiate from many of Lincoln's quoted quips and jests, especially
those from early in his career. For example, he made a humorous
speech in Congress in 1848 about his Black Hawk War "hero[ism]":
he didn't break his sword—"I had none to break, but I bent my
musket pretty badly on one occasion"—and yet he did get bloody
from "struggles with mosquitoes" (I, p. 100). He also readily caught
cold during bivouacs since there was so much of him to make contact with the chilly ground (I, p. 98). While serving for the first time
in the Illinois Legislature, 1834 - 1836, he was one of the "Long
Nine"—nine tall lawmakers whose height totaled fifty-five feet (I,
p. 128). Lincoln's style as a lawyer in the early days—a combination

of rough-and-tumble action and witty story-telling—is detailed graphically (I, pp. 167 - 69, 171 - 72). His love letters to Mary S. Owens are humorously said to have been "filled . . . with arguments going to show that she had better not marry him!" (I, p. 192; X, p. 420). Nicolay and Hay report that Lincoln had such a reputation for "extraordinary wit or humor" that jokes "as old as Howleglass or Rabelais" were often attributed to him (I, p. 306; see also I, p. 308). They note that Lincoln overpowered Douglas during their early debate, on October 3, 1854, at Springfield, partly because of his "bubbling humor, . . . perfect temper, . . . 'and then . . . passages of wit' " (I, p. 379).

Nothing much was bubblingly funny for Lincoln as the 1850s wore along. His biographers report that by the summer of 1854 he was a far more serious, less superficially entertaining political force to reckon with, and his jokes accordingly became fewer and fewer—though, still, "Wherever he went he left an ever-widening ripple of smiles, jests, and laughter" (I, p. 372).

Once elected president and inaugurated, Lincoln found the country so divided, would-be rebels so vocal, and patriots so hushed, that "in Lincoln's own forcible simile, sinners were 'calling the righteous to repentance' " (III, p. 443). Once the Civil War had started, Lincoln suffered chronic trouble with many of his generals, tried to find the golden mean between interfering too much and letting them stagnate too much, and also balanced between issuing somber orders and lightening them with humor. To McClellan, who gave him the most trouble, Lincoln wrote in January, 1862, that "if General McClellan did not want to use the army [the Army of the Potomac] he [Lincoln] would like to borrow it . . ." (V, p. 156). When Hooker in June, 1863, asked permission to lead the Army of the Potomac in an attack against Lee, then about to leave Fredericksburg to invade Pennsylvania, Lincoln dissuaded him at that moment, because of his position, which was expressed in these homely but effective terms: "In one word, I would not take any risk of being entangled upon the river like an ox jumped half over a fence and liable to be torn by dogs front and rear without a fair chance to gore one way or kick the other" (VII, pp. 204 - 05). A month later, after Meade had defeated Lee at Gettysburg, Lincoln without delay urged his general on in bitterly humorous terms: "Call no council of war. It is proverbial that councils of war never fight . . ." (VII, p. 277).

When toward the end Lincoln met with Stephens and other

Confederate leaders at Hampton Roads in February, 1865, and was twitted, in the course of fruitless discussions, to the effect that Charles I of England had been wise enough to parley with people in arms against him, Lincoln wittily replied, "I do not profess to be posted in history. . . . All I distinctly recall about the case of Charles I. is that he lost his head" (X, p. 126).

In their superb essay, "Lincoln's Fame," with which their long biography closes, Nicolay and Hay definitively comment thus: "Many of his phrases form part of the common speech of mankind. It is true that in his writings the range of subjects is not great. . . . But the range of treatment is remarkably wide; it runs from the wit, the gay humor, the florid eloquence of his stump speeches to the marvelous sententiousness and brevity of the letter to Greeley [August 22, 1862] and the address at Gettysburg, and the sustained and lofty grandeur of the Second Inaugural" (X, pp. 351 - 52). In their list of aspects of Lincoln's style, his biographers accord first place to "this saving grace" of humor.

Northern butts of the authors' own barbs include politicians who disagree with Lincoln and also his generals who cannot seem to follow his orders or suggestions. Thus, disaffected New York Governor Horatio Seymour, a Democrat, once "made a long and eloquent speech full of abstract devotion to the Union and of denunciation of all the measures that had hitherto been taken to save it" (IX, p. 256). The career of Chase after Lincoln named him chief justice of the Supreme Court is mercilessly castigated (IX, pp. 395 - 402 *passim*). Examples are too numerous to quote in which the authors' sarcasm withers the laurels of Buell, Frémont, Halleck, and especially McClellan. In a uniquely bitter passage, Nicolay and Hay observe that McClellan "always regarded bad weather as exclusively injurious to him, and never to the other side" (V, p. 414). An effective rhetorical device is the sarcastic contrasting of an energetic commander and one devoted, as McClellan is said to have been, to "amiable inertia" (VI, p. 175). Thus, after Grant had been named as McClellan's replacement, he dispatched a message to Washington expressing gratitude for reinforcements instead of sullenly demanding more and more while preparing to retreat: "Nothing like this had ever before been received from a commander of the Army of the Potomac; a man was now in charge of affairs who respected the Government behind him more than the enemy in front" (VIII, p. 390).[20]

Confederate generals and politicians also are sliced with invec-

tive. Beauregard, Bragg, Early, and especially Hood are frequent
victims. But, of all the Confederate officials, Davis suffers the most
under the lash of sarcasm. His military ability is continually ridiculed; his "gift of never writing to Johnston without infuriating
him" (VIII, p. 327) is laughed at; his amour propre is reviled (IX, p.
452); and his executive logic is lambasted, for example, in this
manner: "Jefferson Davis was strongly addicted to political con-
tradictions, but we must suppose even his cross-eyed philosophy
capable of detecting that a negro willing to fight in slavery in
preference to fighting in freedom was not a very safe reliance for
Southern independence" (X, p. 200).

Other sarcastic passages beg for extended quotation, but exigencies of space forbid.[21] Therefore a final example must suffice. After
paraphrasing gory promises by secret conspirators in the North "to
shed the last drop of their blood to abolish" Lincoln's tyrannical
régime in Washington, the authors drily note: "Shedding the last
drop of one's blood is a comparatively easy sacrifice—it is shedding
the first drop that costs" (VIII, p. 13).[22]

VII   *Stylistic Elements*

The literary style displayed by Nicolay and Hay in their *Lincoln*
has been almost sufficiently indicated, but a few of their minor
features should be briefly noted: their occasional propensity to pon-
tificate in generalizations; their figurative, epithetical, and military
diction; their imperfect control of grammar and syntax; a few
curious idioms; and their too infrequent revelation of a dramatic
and pictorial sense.

Generalizations include ones dealing with military and political
matters, for example, the following: two to one is "the proper
proportion which should always obtain between an army of invasion
. . . and an army of defense" (IX, p. 27), and "violence of
speech . . . [is] no guarantee of political consistency" (X, p. 316).
The authors generalize on the American temperament, as though
they were partly addressing a non-American audience. Thus,
typically, Americans have a "comic brightness . . . in difficult circumstances" (VI, p. 219), "are quick to detect the ludicrous in any
event" (IX, p. 79), are "not especially gifted with the scenic sense"
(X, p. 315), and so on (see also IV, pp. 133, VII, 358).

The authors praise Lincoln's "peculiar imagery" (VI, p. 265) and
occasionally quote it, but their own figurative language through this

whole vast work is almost uniformly hackneyed. Ninety percent of it concerns animals, bees, birds, cobwebs, cups, fire, fruit, ghosts, shadows, thunder and lightning, water, and winds. Inept politicians and diplomats draw their best figurative fire. Thus, in 1864 France gave Confederate envoy John Slidell nothing but verbal encouragement: "When one is consoling a troublesome suitor, whose requests are denied beforehand, words cost little"; meanwhile, turncoat C. L. Vallandigham's blandishments are countered by Sherman's capture of Atlanta: "so close together came bane and antidote" (IX, pp. 155, 351).

Nicolay and Hay frequently add sparkle to their prose by little epithets, the purpose of which is usually to demean. Thus, Lincoln's first teachers are mostly "backwoods dominies"; fly-by-night bogus legislators in Kansas in the 1850s are "migratory Solons" (I, pp. 34, 415); unwashed would-be conspirators in the North during the Civil War are "rural Catalines" (VIII, p. 13); threats of retaliation issued by desperate rebel leaders are ineffectual "crimson edicts" (VII, p. 454), while such gasconaders are labeled "Hotspurs of the South" too often to tally here.

Military diction from the pens of noncombatants often rings false; but, since Nicolay and Hay did their homework well, the result is a thoroughly credible handling of a special vocabulary. Appropriately and unaffectedly used are at least the following: "abatis," "angle," "brush back the pickets," "contravallation," "disgarnished of troops," "enfilade," "flying sappers," *morale*, "redan," "refused flank," "spiteful fire," "take in reverse," and "turn the line." Comments about the joy of battle, however, do seem out of place here. The authors strive for military objectivity and bestow equal praise on common soldiers and sailors of both sides. But they invariably betray their understandable partiality to the Northern side, even in battle descriptions, especially when they employ, as they often do, such revealing pronouns as "we" and "our." Moreover, although they steadfastly follow Lincoln's lead in denying the Confederacy political or diplomatic recognition, they forget at one point and call that band of revolting states "a country" (IX, p. 264).

No author's grammar and syntax can possibly strike every reader as perfect. Although Nicolay and Hay are exceedingly smooth and are usually quite correct, they reveal their human imperfections once in a while. The following is perhaps the most badly composed sentence in the entire work: "He [Norman B. Judd] immediately took [Allan] Pinkerton with him to Mr. Lincoln's room at the Continental Hotel, to whom the whole story was repeated, and where Judd advised that . . ." (III, pp. 307 - 08). Absence of parallelism is hardly a mortal sin, but such writing as the following is nonetheless faulty: "President Lincoln's message was received not only with marks of approbation, but that clause of it which proposed to make the war short and decisive, and to raise an army of four hundred thousand men for the purpose, was greeted with hearty applause." Dangling modifiers appear dozens of times. Thus, of Frémont—"As Senator for a brief term, his votes proved . . . As Presidential candidate . . . in 1856, his name had broadened . . ." (IV, pp. 375, 401). In one sentence, a dangling gerund combines with an affected literary double negative grotesquely: "In studying this unofficial peace mission . . . it will not be uninteresting to . . ." (IX, pp. 206 - 07). Even more negative is this: "Although it cannot be denied that it is not . . . judicious to assign to a general in the field a subordinate who is distasteful to him, we cannot but think that too much has been made of this want of harmony between McClernand and Grant . . ." (VII, p. 141). Many examples might be offered to illustrate the authors' habit of using "and who" or "but which" without using the first "who" or "which." Sufficiently indicative is the following pair of examples: "This was F. W. Pickens, a revolutionist . . . and who . . . had been . . . ," and "Here was a most portentous complication, not of Lincoln's own creating, but which he must . . ." (III, pp. 1 - 2, 378). The authors also employ the useless introductory "There" rather too often, as in this example: "There were many vague charges of improper conduct made by prejudiced persons . . . , but there was never any proof brought forward . . ." (VIII, p. 306). The redundant second "that" is rare but does exist in Nicolay and Hay, as in the following: ". . . he issued a proclamation saying that while he believed it would have been a wise and humane policy to produce a judicial decision, . . . that the failure to do this in no way justified any violent opposition . . ." (VII, p. 37).

The historians use three idioms that grate slightly. One is the construction "so late as" such-and-such a date, instead of "as late as." Another is the meaningless phrase "more or less." And the third is " - ing" in almost archaic forms, as in the following: "[General Montgomery C.] Meigs was about starting for church . . ." (III, p. 436), and "a road was at the same time building from Kentucky . . ." (VIII, p. 170).

This historical narrative might have been improved if the authors had chosen more often to dramatize and pictorialize moments in their epic account. To be sure, they occasionally thrill the reader by scenic renderings of such events as Lee's forces streaming forward, Vicksburg eerily lighted by burning buildings, and Sherman taking in the view at Chattanooga. In addition, Nicolay and Hay repeat themselves on occasion (notice the repetitious description of needles, for a tiny example, in IV, pp. 42, 51), though in general their repetitions are minimal and their transitions—both temporaral and geographical—are managed with consummate skill. As historian M. F. Force complains in a passage sympathetically quoted by Nicolay and Hay, "A combat made up of numberless separate encounters of detached portions of broken lines, continually shifting position and changing direction in the forest and across ravines, filling an entire day, is almost incapable of a connected narrative" (V, p. 324).

VIII *Conclusion*

It has been shown that John G. Nicolay and John Hay did not undertake to narrate merely one battle, as Force tried in his modest book on Shiloh (Pittsburg Landing). Instead, in *Abraham Lincoln: A History* they presented a well-researched, deeply felt, and artistically composed portrait of America's most embattled president against a historical backdrop which highlights diplomatic, political, military, and personal events of panoramic sweep and variety.

Their work drew upon varied biographical and historical sources. Their treatment of Lincoln's presidency is priceless because of their intimate association with the Great Emancipator. Their writing has been of enormous value to the best biographers of Lincoln after them, especially John T. Morse, Jr., Ida M. Tarbell, Lord Charnwood, Albert J. Beveridge, Carl Sandburg, Benjamin P. Thomas, and James G. Randall. It would be interesting but also beyond the scope of this study to trace the influence of early biographers on Nicolay and Hay, to recount the popular and critical reception of their ten-volume work, and to show its specific influence upon later biographers of Lincoln—including those who fail to acknowledge their indebtedness.[23] It is obvious that Lincoln's two secretaries collected many of his letters, speeches, and papers so energetically that later editors are in their debt.[24] It may be added in closing that modern historians of the Civil War have corrected

19

certain military and naval facts, figures, and especially inter-pretations offered by Nicolay and Hay,[25] but that few authors have demonstrated a more comprehensive grasp of the four-year holocaust, especially as it related to concomitant diplomatic and political considerations. And it goes without saying that no one ever wrote about Abraham Lincoln with more devotion to that unique American.

CHAPTER 8

Addresses *and Summary*

I   *Hay's* Addresses

IN 1906, the year after John Hay had died, his friends
assembled twenty-six of his best speeches, including four that
personal circumstances had prevented his delivering, and put them
into a small volume augmented by his 1890 *Century* essay entitled
"Life in the White House in the Time of Lincoln," an 1899 letter
about international copyright, and his Clarence King eulogy, which
had appeared in the 1904 Century Association *Clarence King
Memoirs*. Most of Hay's addresses are political in content, a few
concern literary figures and subjects, and several may be classified
as miscellaneous.

Although his political career had begun in the 1870s, his earliest
speeches published in *Addresses of John Hay* date from 1897, when
Hay became ambassador to England.[1] His last published speech
was delivered in October, 1904. Two others, written for delivery in
December, 1904, were never given. His political speeches are
sometimes historical, as, for example, when he deals with Benjamin
Franklin's diplomatic brilliance in France or when he sketches "Fifty Years of the Republican Party." They may be occasional, as when
he celebrates Independence Day in London in 1897 and again a
year later. They can be frankly partisan, as when he lauds the dead
McKinley or the vital Roosevelt. They become statesmanlike, as
when he surveys "American Diplomacy," argues for continued
Anglo-American friendship—especially in "A Partnership in
Beneficence"—or jingoistically defines "America's Love of Peace"
shortly after the Spanish-American War, the Boxer Rebellion, and
the Philippine occupation. Hay even seizes chances to talk politics
on occasions that are not political. For example, when Hay was invited to address the Royal Society at its annual dinner in 1897, he
accepted, only to explain cleverly that whereas victories for some
groups in war, diplomacy, or trade are often defeats for others, a

120

scientific conquest benefits all; then he added that Anglo-American bonds should be drawn even closer—presumably to produce more victories of various sorts, including scientific ones.

In all of his political addresses, Hay was a thoroughly loyal American and Republican party member. He usually accorded generous praise to the Southern side of the unforgotten Civil War; but, when he remembered Lincoln's agonies, he fanned old sectional embers unnecessarily. He advocated peace through commercial strength and Anglo-American harmony. With never a doubt, he asserted America's destined right to expand and influence in perpetuity: "A country growing so fast must have elbow-room—must have its share of the sunshine."[2] The subject admits no debate or compromise: America and England epitomize and must therefore promulgate liberty, righteousness, and progress everywhere. In no speech did Hay so much as imply either the existence of legitimately disaffected minority groups in the United States or the inevitability of an eventual contraction of American commercial imperialism into the image of an "ugly American."

The literary speeches of Hay are more palatable today, but their subjects are even less controversial now than they were when he delivered them. He extols Omar Khayyám and his British translator Edward FitzGerald, if briefly and in terms that now seem too general. The popularity of this little lecture was phenomenal, for, in Hay's lifetime, it was reprinted in various forms at least a dozen times. Today the main value of Hay's "Omar Khayyám" lies in the light it casts on his own nature: Hay comes through here as gentle, poetic, stoical, and self-effacing.[3]

The same estimate applies to his Westminster Abbey speech on the occasion of the unveiling of Sir Walter Scott's bust. Hay notes that Scott "has received the uncritical, ungrudging love of grateful millions" (p. 58), and then he is himself uncritical in expressing his devotion to the novelist. Hay also notes that Scott had no influence on America's political and material evolution, but then he ingeniously adds that New World pioneers find in his works characters from the rugged Scottish past of a sort that they themselves will become in the eyes of their own descendants. Far from concealing the rude simplicity of his own forebears, Hay takes delight in telling his appreciative British auditors that his father, "a pioneer of Kentucky," and his friends used to await with keen excitement the arrival of the latest Waverley novel at "the principal post-town of the region" (pp. 54, 55). Equally palatable to another

English group was Hay's praise of Robert Browning's "intellectual
energy and moral earnestness," as displayed in his poetry, "which
taught the innate dignity of human nature,—its right always to
learn, always to aspire" (pp. 99, 100).

Surely the least effective lecture Hay ever prepared about a
literary topic was in praise of Edmund Clarence Stedman on the occasion of that nearly forgotten American poet's seventieth birthday
in 1903. Virtually everything Hay said about Stedman and the
poetic calling would appear to be precisely the reverse of applicable
now: youth is uncertain, whereas those in old age are sure of the
future; when the sun is declining in the west, all shadows are left
behind; Stedman is brilliant and also admirably industrious; in all
his business dealings, he maintained "the most stainless honor" (p.
230); his prophetic poem on John Brown has deservedly lived in
Hay's mind for forty years; and other great American writers of the
time include Bayard Taylor, Richard Henry Stoddard, George
Henry Boker, Thomas Bailey Aldrich, and William Dean Howells.
Significantly, Hay failed to mention Stedman's work as a critical
editor—almost the only literary accomplishment by which Stedman
is known today.

Miscellaneous addresses and brief, informal speeches contain
comments Hay made in praise of New Orleans, "All through my
childhood . . . a realm of faery, a land of dreams" (p. 205); in
praise of the University of California at Berkeley, where Hay
accepted an honorary degree in 1901; in praise of the Grand Army
of the Republic during its 1902 encampment in Washington, D.C.;
and in shrewd praise of Chicago for its unboasted strength, sym-
bolic position in America's heartland, and tendency toward
"democracy, freedom and light" (p. 199). When Hay received
honorary degrees at Princeton University (1900) and Harvard
University (1902), he improved each occasion by mentioning not
only the brilliance of the White House incumbent (first McKinley
and then Roosevelt) but also his own total unworthiness.

Firmer in tone is Hay's address to the Press Parliament of the
World, at the Louisiana Purchase Exposition, St. Louis, 1904. This
speech, which is one of his most representative ones, begins with
pontifical generalizations, delivered in a mock-modest tone, about
the power of the press, the timely decline of "personal government"
(p. 243), and the potency of public opinion. Hay then turns to
autobiographical materials, rather graciously but in prose which today might best be characterized as "corny." Next he rings some

effective changes on the subject of American manifest destiny—"a
cosmic tendency" (p. 250)—and then turns specifically to the
Louisiana Purchase as proof that fate has smiled upon "the Eagle in
his marvelous flight" (p. 253). Somewhat smug comments follow in
asseveration of America's love of righteousness, justice, and
humanity everywhere. Imagery so trite as to sound almost ironic
tells of "the illuminating blaze of light which the press each morning radiates on the universe!" (p. 254); but this statement is quickly
followed by sincere, accurate praise of the telegraph which sparks
this "blaze." Then Hay comments with almost Olympian detach-
ment about the varied ingenuity which has produced miraculous in-
dustrial products displayed in the Exposition but which also proves
that the result of such ingenuity is invariably the same—success. He
closes by welcoming all visitors in the name of President Roosevelt,
in the face of whose triple potency as "writer, soldier, and
statesman" (pp. 258 - 59) any speaker would have to be modest.[4]

Literary references are not so frequent in Hay's addresses as we
might have guessed. In addition to writers already mentioned, Hay
names only once Virgil, Milton, Poe, Ruskin, and Tolstoy; and he
speaks only twice of Whitman—who is most loyally identified once
as "my old friend" (p. 90)—and of Henry Adams, who is simply
defined as "the great historian" (p. 67). Most surprising seems to be
the praise given by Hay to Tolstoy, wondrously lauded for his solu-
tion to the world's woes—religion, which word the great Russian
"speaks . . . as it has been given him to speak it, and as no other
living man could have done" (p. 312).

What personal traits does Hay reveal in his addresses? Judging
from them, we might conclude that their writer was learned,
modest or perhaps only apparently so, weary of it all but resolved to
play out the game graciously and decorously, witty but probably
less so than he once was or thinks he now is, a bit sycophantic, and
as aged as Tithonus. The two personal attributes that most frequently appear are modesty and weariness. Yet, such is the complexity of Hay's personality behind these speeches that we can
glimpse the lurking possibility that the speaker may be a prince or a
genius in disguise who is forced to assume a modesty that his
hidden worth would decry if given permission, and, furthermore,
that though tired unto death, the fellow remembers his boyhood on
the Mississippi River with undiminished glee and would shuck his
robes of state and go skating there again if given half a chance.

It must be frankly added that Hay the writer is not at his best in most of these addresses. Usually the subject was assigned to him. Since he often went in someone else's place—sometimes, even the president's—his position may have affected his style. Moreover, the circumstances of their delivery forced upon most of these addresses more gravity than Hay probably ever wanted his personal spoken words to have. He was a shy and diffident man, especially before masses of people. Therefore his diction is often pretentious, unnatural, even oddly biblical. His imagery is occasionally embarrassing. His wit is often a little forced. Atop these stylistic infelicities may be found some of Hay's old poetic clichés. Thus—"It is meet that at this stage of our journey we . . ." (p. 264). The memory of Clarence King is "a souvenir so delightful" (p. 346). Hay brings his Berkeley audience "some of his [McKinley's] garnered sheaves of experience and of wisdom" (p. 186). Witnesses of American honesty are "like them that dream" (p. 287). Journalists "have won the praise of earth and the blessing of Heaven since the morning of time" (p. 317). The beauty of the 1901 Buffalo Pan American Exposition enables "the many to fill their days with gladness and their nights with music" (p. 132). At the end of the Civil War, the Union Army "melts away into the vaster body of the nation, as the foam-crested sunlit wave melts back into the profound depths of the ocean" (p. 212). Meanwhile, " . . . young writers [in America in 1898] . . . are beginning to flame in the forehead of the morning sky" (p. 95).

In addition, the following awkwardnesses, all taken from Hay's *Addresses*, sound familiar to readers of his *Lincoln:* "But there has been more noise made . . ." (p. 296); "devoted to ends more or less noble" (p. 57); "the scaffolding was building for John Brown" (p. 232); "Breathing a poisoned air from his birth, moral health was impossible to him [the Duke of Orléans]" (p. 11); and finally, "A position of complete independence is not incompatible with relations involving not friendship alone . . ." (p. 122).

II *Brief Summary*

John Hay is an unusual figure in American history. His childhood was typical enough, but his chance to go to the East for study put him on the road to so-called success and therefore infected him with aspects of the American Dream. Later, his talent and attractiveness stood him in good stead, and his friendship with Lincoln's secretary, John G. Nicolay, altered his life. After hard work on the White

House staff, followed by diplomatic work in Europe, Hay returned home restlessly, married a woman of fabulous wealth, and let his deep-seated love of ease triumph over his Middle Western devotion to work and a fair shake for all. He became a little effete and super-cilious, but he also remained disquieted and self-deprecating. Successes came too easily. He began to realize that nothing but passive pleasures meant much to him.

Hay accomplished a great deal in the realm of international statesmanship, and the world may be a better place today because of his efforts as secretary of state. But after each coup, he permitted others to take the credit while he kept promising his superiors, his peers, his subordinates, and his family that he would soon quit and "be comfortably dead."[5]

Hay's successes in the realm of public affairs are well known. The man was a scintillating ambassador, and then the author of the Open Door Policy and of the treaty making possible the Panama Canal. His successes in literature should be better known than they are. His poetry is competent, and the few pieces he wrote in Pike County dialect are more than that. His book on Spain has moments of acuteness and eloquence. His fiction is smoothly entertaining and occasionally thrilling; it anticipates later work in the realms of inter-national manners, middle-border realism, and antilabor or at least procapital naturalism. Hay's collaboration with Nicolay on their biography-history of Lincoln and the Civil War not only is priceless but also has been incalculably influential. Hay's public speeches are mostly unpalatable today, but they were listened to with an eagerness bordering on awe.

One of Hay's best accomplishments was his friendship with many literary people who were professionally more ambitious than he. Anyone who was a lifelong friend of Henry Adams, Mark Twain, William Dean Howells, Henry James, and Walt Whitman must have been unique. Hay encouraged the best in them all. He could afford to be generous, but others similarly capable have been in-different. Hay's joys were too passive—being with his family, reading, traveling—and they hint at his intermittent morbidity; but, between vacations, Hay produced many volumes of writing—especially if we include his belletristic private cor-respondence.

The ultimate critical comment about Hay must include negatives. He was often lazy. His first poetry was his best. He chose not to pursue his two main fictive themes—Americans in Europe and the harshness of Middle Western rural life. The year 1890, the date his most ambitious work, *Abraham Lincoln: A History,* was published, was precisely the date that one of the most exciting decades in American literature began.[6] Hay had the means and talent to become part of that intellectual ferment, but he failed to do so. And in 1905, when an Asian power, Japan, first defeated a partly European one, Russia, and thus sounded a new note in international diplomacy, Hay, who had helped to make such a change possible, escaped by death from the obligation of entering that brave new world.

Notes and References

Chapter One

1. John Hay, *Dr. Charles Hay . . .* (New York, 1884), p. 4; Henry Adams, ed., *Letters of John Hay and Extracts from Diary* (Washington, 1908), I, iv; Tyler Dennett, *John Hay: From Poetry to Politics* (New York, 1933), pp. 2, 8, 9.

2. Lorenzo Sears, *John Hay: Author and Statesman* (New York, 1914), p. 3; Dennett, *Hay*, pp. 3 - 9. John G. Nicolay and John Hay describe the founding of Transylvania University in *Abraham Lincoln: A History* (New York, 1890), I, 15 - 16. Farnham is the name of the hero of John Hay's anonymously published novel *The Bread-Winners*.

3. Sears, *Hay*, p. 4; Dennett, *Hay*, pp. 10 - 12; Adams, ed., *Letters of Hay*, I, iv - v. Hay describes the Des Moines River in flood in his 1869 short story "The Foster-Brothers."

4. Sears, *Hay*, pp. 7, 9; A. S. Chapman, "The Boyhood of John Hay," *Century*, LXXVIII (June, 1909), 445 - 47; Dennett, *Hay*, pp. 15 - 17, 19, 32. Hay dropped his middle name of Milton, derived from his uncle, while in college, where he thought his poetic aspirations would be ill served by it—Dennett, *Hay*, p. 14n. For details on Milton Hay and Abraham Lincoln, see Nicolay and Hay, *Lincoln*, I, 167 - 69, 171 - 72, 214n.

5. Sears, *Hay*, pp. 7 - 22 *passim;* William Roscoe Thayer, *The Life and Letters of John Hay* (Boston, 1915), I, 35n, 43 - 47 *passim;* Chapman, "Boyhood of Hay," pp. 446, 449; *A Poet in Exile: Early Letters of John Hay*, ed. Caroline Ticknor (Boston and New York, 1910), p. 23; *A College Friendship: A Series of Letters from John Hay to Hannah Angell*, ed. Amy A. C. Montague (Boston, 1938), p. 41; Dennett, *Hay*, p. 22. Hay in his novel *The Bread-Winners: A Social Study*, ed. Charles Vandersee (New Haven, 1973), p. 170, mentions hashish in a curious passage. Hay was sycophantic toward Mrs. Whitman; see *A Poet in Exile*, pp. 14, 20, 25, 40, 43, 46.

6. Thayer, *Life of Hay*, I, 59; *Poet in Exile*, p. 23; Dennett, *Hay*, p. 32.

7. Hay got the job with Lincoln mainly through Uncle Milton—Jesse W. Weik, *The Real Lincoln: A Portrait* (Boston and New York, 1922), p. 284.

8. Thayer, *Life of Hay*, I, 86 - 89; Dennett, *Hay*, p. 35; Francis B. Heitman, *Historical Register and Dictionary of the United States Army* (Washington, 1903), I, 514. It is amusing that Hay in *Castilian Days* (Boston, 1871), pp. 394 - 95, inveighs against rapid promotions in the Spanish Army in 1868 - 69.

9. Hay to William Henry Herndon, from Paris, September 5, 1866, reproduced in a pamphlet from the original in a collection of Lincolniana formed by Herndon and in the possession of Gabriel Wells—copy in the John Hay Collection in the Brown University Library.

10. Nicolay and Hay, *Lincoln*, VIII, 10 - 11, 282 - 85, IX, 184 - 200; William M. Lamers, *The Edge of Glory: A Biography of General William S. Rosecrans, U.S.A.* (New York, 1961), p. 421; Henry Luther Stoddard, *Horace Greeley: Printer, Editor, Crusader* (New York, 1946), pp. 215 - 16, 226. Nicolay and Hay severely criticize Greeley in *Lincoln*, III, 253n, 258, VI, 152, IX, 184 - 200 *passim*. See also *Lincoln and the Civil War in the Diaries and Letters of John Hay* (New York, 1939), pp. 55 - 65, 159 - 64, 188 - 94.

11. *Lincoln in Diaries of Hay*, pp. 51, 99, 139, 211; Nicolay and Hay, *Lincoln*, X, 301; Thayer, *Life of Hay*, I, 147.

12. *Register of Officers and Agents, Civil, Military, and Naval, in the Service of the United States, on the Thirtieth September, 1865* (Washington, 1866), p. 4; *Letters of Hay*, I, 253 - 54; *Lincoln in Diaries of Hay*, p. 254. On French, Spanish, and English military adventures in Mexico during the Civil War, see Nicolay and Hay, *Lincoln*, VI, 30 - 48 *passim*, 62 - 63, 77, 82. On Napoleon III and the Confederate States, see *ibid.*, IV, 269, V, 41, VII, 398 - 403, 410 - 23 *passim*, VIII, 265 - 80 *passim*, 285, IX, 139 - 41, 153, X, 99.

13. *Letters of Hay*, I, 275 - 88; *Lincoln in Diaries of Hay*, p. 280; Thayer, *Life of Hay*, I, 315 - 26; Dennett, *Hay*, pp. 65 - 67.

14. *Letters of Hay*, I, 295 - 367 *passim*; Thayer, *Life of Hay*, I, 280 - 311 *passim*; Dennett, *Hay*, p. 64; *Lincoln in Diaries of Hay*, pp. 287 - 95.

15. *Lincoln in Diaries of Hay*, p. 293.

16. *Letters of Hay*, I, 372 - 84; *Lincoln in Diaries of Hay*, p. 300; Thayer, *Life of Hay*, I, 315 - 26; Dennett, *Hay*, pp. 65 - 67.

17. *Lincoln in Diaries of Hay*, p. 324.

18. Dennett, *Hay*, p. 59.

19. Hay wrote Hannah Angell of his "dry, barren agony of soul" following Ellsworth's death—*College Friendship*, p. 61. See also Hay, *Castilian Days*, p. 157; Nicolay and Hay, *Lincoln*, III, 290n, IV, 312 - 14, 320. Hay remembered Ellsworth in a 1902 speech—see *Addresses of John Hay* (New York, 1906), p. 146.

20. William Easton Louttit, Jr., "John Hay: A Short List of His Writings," in Dennett, *Hay*, p. 451; George Monteiro, "John Hay's Short Fiction," *Studies in Short Fiction*, VIII (Fall, 1971), 543 - 44. Two installments of *Castilian Days*, which appeared as the last two chapters of the work in book form, Hay published, in reverse order and pseudonymously (as by Richard West), in the *Atlantic Monthly* XXV (March, 1870), 368 - 76, and (May, 1870), 626 - 32.

21. Jacob Blanck, "John Milton Hay," *Bibliography of American Literature*, IV (New Haven and London, 1963), p. 40; *American Literary Magazine and Lecture Season*, September, 1871, p. 36.

22. Dennett, *Hay*, p. 71.

23. Thayer, *Life of Hay*, I, 330 - 34 *passim;* Dennett, *Hay,* pp. 88 - 89; Ralph Ray Fahrney, *Horace Greeley and the* Tribune *in the Civil War* (Cedar Rapids, Iowa, 1936), pp. 155 - 72. After writing about Greeley's critical letter to Lincoln following the Union defeat at First Bull Run (Manassas), Nicolay and Hay, in *Lincoln,* IV, 367, conclude thus: "letters like that . . . made him [Lincoln] sigh at the strange weakness of human character." On no revealed authority, Sears, in *Hay,* p. 37, says that "It was years before he [Greeley] forgave Hay his companionship" on the Niagara Falls peace mission.

24. George Monteiro, "John Hay as Reporter: Special Correspondence on the Great Chicago Fire," *Books at Brown,* XXII (1968), 81 - 94; Dennett, *Hay,* p. 89; George Monteiro, *Henry James and John Hay: The Record of a Friendship* (Providence, 1965), p. 11. For Howells on Hay's *Castilian Days,* see Kenton J. Clymer, *John Hay: The Gentleman as Diplomat* (Ann Arbor, 1975), pp. 7, 215.

25. Dennett, *Hay,* p. 77. Moreover, in *Castilian Days,* though popular with the undiscerning public, Hay began to fear he had gone too far in criticizing Roman Catholicism and monarchism in Spain. He later branded himself as "a very stout and irresponsible Protestant and Republican" for writing as he had in the book—quoted in Dennett, *Hay,* p. 82.

26. *Ibid.,* pp. 96 - 97; *Letters of Hay,* II, 13, 14, 21; *Poet in Exile,* pp. 18 - 19; *Addresses,* p. 221. For a picture of Clara Hay, see Dennett, *Hay,* opp. p. 98.

27. For information on ruthless Amasa Stone, see Dennett, *Hay,* pp. 99 - 102, 109; Allan Nevins, *John D. Rockefeller: The Heroic Age of American Enterprise* (New York, 1940), I, 388 - 395 *passim,* 443, II, 405; Vandersee, "Introduction" to Hay, *Bread-Winners,* p. 34. For a picture of Stone, see Frederic Cople Jaher, "Industrialism and the American Aristocrat: A Social Study of John Hay and His Novel, *The Bread-Winners," Journal of Illinois State Historical Society,* LXV (1972), 72.

28. Dennett, *Hay,* pp. 97, 98. For later high praise of Clara Hay, see Abigail Adams Homans, *Education by Uncles* (Boston, 1966), pp. 95 - 96. For mild implicit criticism, see Clymer, *Hay,* pp. 9, 89, 114, 242.

29. Dennett, *Hay,* p. 123. Howells and Mark Twain said the same thing—see Howells, "John Hay in Literature," *North American Review,* CLXXI (September, 1905), 351; Mark Twain's *Correspondence with Henry Huttleston Rogers 1893 - 1909,* ed. Lewis Leary (Berkeley and Los Angeles, 1969), p. 552.

30. Dennett, *Hay,* p. 126.

31. *Letters of Hay,* II, 55; Theodore Clarke Smith, *The Life and Letters of James Abram Garfield* (New Haven, 1925), pp. 1069 - 71. Hay campaigned well for Garfield—see Ernest Samuels, *Henry Adams: The Major Phase* (Cambridge, Mass., 1964), p. 401; Clymer, *Hay,* pp. 50 - 51. Friends were sorry to see the Hays leave Washington—see *The Letters of Mrs. Henry Adams,* ed. Ward Thoron (Boston, 1936), pp. 274, 286.

32. Royal Cortissoz, *The Life of Whitelaw Reid* (London, 1921), II, 70 -
77. An observer contrasted the two editors: "The rule of the paper under
Reid was that of whips, with Hay it was that of scorpions"—John Russell
Young, *Men and Memories: Personal Reminiscences* (New York, 1901), pp.
460 - 61. See also Clymer, *Hay*, p. 20.

33. Thayer, *Life of Hay*, II, 8; Dennett, *Hay*, 107n; Blanck,
Bibliography of American Literature, IV, 43. Hay evidently gave Matthew
Arnold a copy of his novel when the two met in Cleveland in January,
1884—see George Monteiro, "Matthew Arnold and John Hay: Three Unpublished Letters," *Notes and Queries*, X, n.s. (February, 1966), 66 - 67.

34. *Letters of Mrs. Adams*, p. 450; Ernest Samuels, *Henry Adams: The
Middle Years* (Cambridge, Mass., 1958), p. 459. Hay later spoke from experience of the dangers of "luxury which could enervate mind or
body"—*Addresses*, p. 143.

35. Orison Swett Marden, "John Hay Stands Next to McKinley,"
Success, II (December 9, 1899), 20. Hay evidently did not deny this story or
otherwise silence Marden, who repeated his revelation in an expanded
sketch of Hay in *Talks with Great Workers* (New York, 1901), p. 136.

36. *Letters of Hay*, II, 22, 26; Thayer, *Life of Hay*, II, 23.

37. *Letters of Hay*, II, 87. Compare Nicolay and Hay, "Authors'
Preface," *Lincoln*, I, xiii: ". . . we have known no allegiance but to the
truth." However, Paul M. Angle, in *A Shelf of Lincoln Books: A Critical,
Selective Bibliography of Lincolniana* (New Brunswick, N.J., 1946), pp.
34 - 35, says that Nicolay and Hay were sufficiently frank.

38. Quoted in pastiche by Emanuel Hertz, *The Hidden Lincoln: From
the Letters and Papers of William H. Herndon* (New York, 1938), p. 15.
David Donald, in *Lincoln's Herndon* (New York, 1948), pp. 311, 347, con-
curs in Herndon's adverse assessment.

39. Sears, *Hay*, p. 64. Roy P. Basler, highly knowledgeable Lincoln expert, is of the personal opinion, expressed orally to me, that Nicolay was
more responsible for the organization and execution of *Lincoln* than is
generally known.

40. Margaret Leech, *Reveille in Washington: 1860 - 1865* (New York
and London, 1941), p. 443; Thayer, *Life of Hay*, II, 40.

41. *Letters of Hay*, II, 174, 183. In reality, Hay enjoyed ample research
and editorial assistance—see Dennett, *Hay*, p. 151. Much evidence in the
John G. Nicolay Papers, Library of Congress (especially Box 5, 1890
materials), leads me to believe that Hay permitted his older colleague to
handle most of the problems—including that of indexing—which arose
before book publication.

42. Nicolay Papers, Library of Congress.

43. Dennett, *Hay*, p. 141. The Nicolay Papers, Library of Congress, are
replete with laudatory reviews, encomiums, and courteous queries from
pleased readers.

Chapter Two

1. Sears, *Hay*, p. 20; Dennett, *Hay*, p. 443.
2. *Letters of Henry Adams (1858 - 1891)*, ed. Worthington Chauncey Ford (Boston and New York, 1930), p. 340. For more on the Five of Hearts, see Ford, ed., *Letters of Adams (1858 - 1891)*, p. 335n; Thoron, ed., *Letters of Mrs. Adams*, pp. 238 - 39n; *Henry Adams and His Friends: A Collection of His Unpublished Letters*, ed. Harold Dean Cater (Boston, 1947), pp. xliv, 103; Samuels, *Adams: Middle Years*, pp. 171 - 80, 562.
3. Dennett, *Hay*, p. 161; *Letters of Hay*, II, 98. When Hay's son Adelbert died in 1901, Adams wrote his agonized friend not to give up as he himself had done sixteen years earlier—see Condolence Scrapbook, Hay Collection, Brown. On Adams and his wife, see Otto Friedrich, "Clover and Henry Adams—A Most Unusual Love Story," *Smithsonian*, VIII (April, 1977), 58 - 64, 66 - 67.
4. Dennett, *Hay*, p. 175; *Letters of Hay*, III, 78 - 79. For Adams's replies to Hay, see *Adams and His Friends*, pp. 390 - 93.
5. Dennett, *Hay*, p. 181. Louis Martin Sears, in "John Hay in London, 1897 - 1898," *Ohio Historical Quarterly*, LXV (October, 1956), 356, says baldly that "The mission of John Hay . . . was among the most successful in his country's annals."
6. George W. Smalley, *Anglo-American Memories* (New York and London, 1911), p. 210; see also Lady St. Helier (Mary Jeune), *Memories of Fifty Years* (London, 1909), pp. 311 - 15, and Sears, "Hay in London," p. 374, for proof of Hay's popularity in England.
7. Dennett, *Hay*, p. 187 - 88; Elizabeth Stevenson, *Henry Adams: A Biography* (New York, 1955), pp. 175, 276. On Hay's possible negligence following the *Maine* incident, see Clymer, *Hay*, pp. 114 - 15. Egypt provided Hay with figurative and allusive material used in subsequent speeches—see *Addresses*, pp. 91, 166, 172 - 73.
8. Dennett, *Hay*, p. 195; Thayer, *Life of Hay*, II, 173; James Ford Rhodes, *The McKinley and Roosevelt Administrations, 1897 - 1909* (New York, 1922), pp. 31, 41, 42.
9. Dennett, *Hay*, p. 196. John St. Loe Strachey confirms the fact of Hay's reluctance to leave London for Washington at this time—see *The Adventure of Living: A Subjective Autobiography* (New York and London, 1922), p. 391.
10. Thayer, *Life of Hay*, II, 337; *Letters of Hay*, III, 122. Sears, in "Hay in London," p. 372, says that Hay's "part in the war . . . had indeed been notable."
11. *Addresses*, p. 250.
12. Thayer, *Life of Hay*, II, 338, 339; Dennett, *Hay*, p. 349. Kenton J. Clymer, the most recent scholar to comment on Hay and Roosevelt, intelligently concludes thus: "Hay's entire relationship with Roosevelt

demonstrated Hay's essential ambiguity. If Roosevelt was the preeminent representative of the new century, Hay had a foot in both the old one and the new . . . Hay, . . . although sometimes uncomfortable with Roosevelt's robustness, had little difficulty serving the new president"; *Hay*, pp. 208 - 09, 211.

13. For background on international tensions during Hay's tenure in office, see Barbara W. Tuchman, *The Proud Tower: A Portrait of the World before the War: 1890 - 1914* (New York, 1966), pp. 243 - 72 *passim.*

14. Dennett, *Hay*, pp. 197, 268 - 69; Thayer, *Life of Hay*, II, 186 - 87. For Hay and White, see Allan Nevins, *Henry White: Thirty Years of American Diplomacy* (New York and London, 1930), *passim;* for the Roosevelt-Hay-White relationship, see Raymond A. Esthus, *Theodore Roosevelt and the International Rivalries* (Waltham, Mass., 1970), pp. 17 - 18.

15. Thayer, *Life of Hay*, II, 190 - 92, 199, 214 - 15, 280 - 81; Dennett, *Hay*, pp. 286 - 87. Pauncefote revered Hay—see R. B. Mowat, *The Life of Lord Pauncefote: First Ambassador to the United States* (London, 1929), pp. 125 - 27, 204 - 05, 250.

16. Dennett, *Hay*, pp. 210, 290 - 91. On Hippisley, see Samuel Flagg Bemis, *A Diplomatic History of the United States*, 3rd ed. (New York, 1950), p. 484.

17. Thayer, *Life of Hay*, II, 221; Dennett, *Hay*, p. 241. Hay disputed with Senator Lodge over British concentration camps in South Africa—see *ibid.*, p. 243.

18. *Ibid.*, pp. 268 - 69; Bemis, *Diplomatic History*, p. 474; Thayer, *Life of Hay*, II, 281 - 82; Hay, *Addresses*, p. 123. Adams had vacationed in Samoa, 1890 - 91, and kept Hay informed on the region—see *Adams and His Friends*, pp. 197 - 239 *passim.*

19. Dennett, *Hay*, pp. 238, 242 - 43, 250 - 54 *passim*, 270, 293; Thayer, *Life of Hay*, II, 223. Hay long held venomous opinions of the U.S. Senate, which he regarded as "a mad house" powered by "ignorance and spite, acting upon cowardice"—*ibid.*, II, 176. Hay's loathing is mentioned in almost every important book dealing with the diplomacy of this epoch; for example, see Clymer, *Hay*, pp. 125, 175, 177 - 78, 185, 201.

20. Thayer, *Life of Hay*, II, 227, 228; see also Charles S. Olcott, *The Life of William McKinley* (Boston and New York, 1916), I, 372 - 73.

21. Dennett, *Hay*, p. 293.

22. *Letters of Henry Adams (1892 - 1918)*, ed. Worthington Chauncey Ford (Boston and New York, 1938), p. 281; Arthur F. Berlingause, *Brooks Adams: A Biography* (New York, 1955), p. 206.

23. A. Whitney Griswold, *The Far Eastern Policy of the United States* (New Haven and London, 1962), p. 88; Thomas A. Bailey, *A Diplomatic History of the American People*, 8th ed. (New York, 1969), p. 481; George F. Kennan, *American Diplomacy: 1900 - 1950* (Chicago, 1951), pp. 32, 35 -

37. For confirmation of Kennan's adverse opinion, see Norman A. Graebner, ed., *Ideas and Diplomacy: Readings in the Intellectual Tradition of American Foreign Policy* (New York, 1964), pp. 334 - 46.

24. Dennett, *Hay*, p. 299. See also Clymer, *Hay*, pp. 148 - 53 *passim*.

25. Bemis, *Diplomatic History*, p. 487.

26. Dennett, *Hay*, pp. 304 - 305; Olcott, *Life of McKinley*, II, 242 - 43; Philip C. Jessup, *Elihu Root* (New York, 1938), I, 381; Elsie Porter Meade, *An American Soldier and Diplomat: Horace Porter* (New York, 1927), pp. 253 - 91 *passim*.

27. *Letters of Adams (1892 - 1918)*, p. 289; Thayer, *Life of Hay*, II, 252; Dennett, *Hay*, pp. 306, 436.

28. *Ibid.*, pp. 244 - 45, 257 - 59, 272 - 75.

29. *Ibid.*, pp. 260, 263, 316, 322 - 23, 351 - 52; Thayer, *Life of Hay*, II, 258 - 62; Olcott, *Life of McKinley*, II, 261. Hay later publicly praised McKinley for withdrawing American troops from the Far East—*Addresses*, p. 310.

30. Sears, *Hay*, pp. 101 - 02; Thayer, *Life of Hay*, II, 262 - 65. For clippings of contemporary newspaper accounts, see Condolence Scrapbook, Hay Collection, Brown.

31. *Adams and His Friends*, p. 515. A measure of Hay's renown is suggested by the fact that King Edward VII of England sent a personal note of sympathy—Dennett, *Hay*, p. 233.

32. *Letters of Hay*, III, 229, 230.

33. *Ibid.*, III, 232. H. H. Kohlsaat, in *From McKinley to Harding: Personal Recollections of Our Presidents* (New York and London, 1923), pp. 97 - 99, reports that upon becoming president, Roosevelt thought seriously of naming Elihu Root as secretary of state but was persuaded by Kohlsaat to retain Hay.

34. Richard W. Leopold, in *The Growth of American Foreign Policy: A History* (New York, 1962), p. 110, suggests that Hay was a good secretary of state who would have been a better one if he had both emboldened McKinley and restrained Roosevelt more successfully.

35. The whole letter, dated September 15, 1901, Dennett rightly calls one of Hay's finest—*Hay*, p. 341.

36. Hay privately distrusted Russia—see Dennett, *Hay*, p. 405; A. L. P. Dennis, "John Hay," p. 189, in *The American Secretaries of State and Their Diplomacy*, ed. Samuel Flagg Bemis (New York, 1958); Clymer, *Hay*, pp. 152 - 53, 155. But like a good diplomat, Hay praised Russia in speeches—see, for one example, *Addresses*, p. 317. For the Canadian attitude toward Hay, Salisbury, and the Alaskan question, see Gerald M. Craig, *The United States and Canada* (Cambridge, Mass., 1968), p. 169. On Roosevelt and the Panama Canal, see Howard C. Hill, *Roosevelt and the Caribbean* (Chicago, 1927), p. 45. For more general background, see United States Congress, *The Story of Panama: Hearings on the Rainey*

Resolution before the Committee on Foreign Affairs of the House of Representatives (Washington, 1913), *passim;* Maron J. Simon, *The Panama Affair* (New York, 1971), p. 250.

37. Dennett, *Hay*, pp. 397 - 98. Hay may have had a disfiguring touch of anti-Semitism—*Letters of Hay*, I, 327 - 29; Dennett, *Hay*, p. 397; Kenton J. Clymer, "Anti-Semitism in the Late Nineteenth Century: The Case of John Hay," *American Jewish Historical Quarterly*, LX (June, 1971), 344 - 54; Robert Mane, *Henry Adams on the Road to Chartres* (Cambridge, Mass., 1971), pp. 86 - 88. For Hay's part in official protests against Russian anti-Semitism, see Isadore Singer, *Russia at the Bar of the American People: A Memorial of Kishinev* (New York and London, 1904), pp. 112 -61 *passim*. For Hay's more cavalier, privately implied attitude, see *What Me Befell: The Reminiscences of J. J. Jusserand* (Boston and New York, 1933), pp. 239 - 40, 244. Hay was sympathetic toward Jews in Medieval and Renaissance times but only—it would seem—because vicious treatment of them by the Spanish gave him a chance to vent his antimonarchical, anti-Catholic spleen—see his *Castilian Days*, pp. 193 - 94, 278 - 79, 411.

38. Dennett, *Hay*, pp. 360, 431.

39. *Ibid.*, pp. 361 - 62, 375, 377. Did Hay at this point remember his annoyance at European threats to recognize the Confederate States as early as 1861?—see Nicolay and Hay, *Lincoln*, IV, 266 - 80. For a detailed review of data concerning Hay and the Panamanian revolution, see Clymer, *Hay*, pp. 202 - 08. Clymer comments disparagingly on Hay's "deviousness and two-facedness" at this juncture, on the likelihood that "Hay supported Roosevelt's actions in the Panama revolution," and on the fact that from mid-September, 1903, until the revolution "references to Panamanian affairs rather suspiciously cease in Hay's still extant letters" (pp. 202, 204, 206).

40. Sir Cecil Spring-Rice, British diplomat then in St. Petersburg, advised Hay on Russian difficulties through voluminous letters—see *The Letters and Friendships of Sir Cecil Spring-Rice*, ed. Stephen Gwynn (London, 1929), I, 388 - 440 *passim*.

41. Dennett, *Hay*, pp. 382 - 83. U. S. Congress, *Story of Panama*, pp. 94 - 99, prints the convention Hay and Bunau-Varilla signed on November 18, 1903. For partisan details, see Philippe Bunau-Varilla, *Panama: The Creation, Destruction, and Resurrection* (London, 1913), pp. 160, 350, 367 - 78, 417 - 20, 430 - 31.

42. Thayer, *Life of Hay*, II, 376; *Addresses*, p. 250.

43. Thayer, *Life of Hay*, II, 383 - 84; Dennett, *Hay*, pp. 401 - 02. The Perdicaris-Raisuli episode, suitably complicated militarily and sexually, provided the basis for the 1975 movie *The Wind and the Lion*, in which big John Huston played little John Hay to Brian Keith's Teddy Roosevelt.

44. Thayer, *Life of Hay*, II, 371 - 75 *passim*. Elihu Root, Hay's able successor as secretary of state, concluded the 1908 Root-Takahira executive agreement, which encouraged Japanese imperialism in the Pacific—see

Bemis, *Diplomatic History*, pp. 495 - 97, 680 - 81; L. Ethan Ellis, *A Short History of American Diplomacy* (New York, 1951), p. 323. For details on the cabinet association of Hay and Root, see Jessup, *Root*, I, 379 - 407 *passim*. Esthus is of the opinion that "Roosevelt . . . overrated Root, just as he underrated Hay"; *Roosevelt and International Rivalries*, p. 7.

45. Thayer, *Life of Hay*, II, 399 - 403 *passim;* Dennett, *Hay*, p. 437; Strachey, *Adventure of Living*, p. 396.

46. Thayer, *Life of Hay*, II, 405; Dennett, *Hay*, p. 439.

47. Sears, *Hay*, pp. 103 - 04; Thayer, *Life of Hay*, II, 407; Dennett, *Hay*, p. 439.

48. Thayer, *Life of Hay*, II, 407, 408; *Letters of Hay*, III, 350. Poignantly, the sentence quoted above and beginning "I have had success . . ." originally read "I have success. . . ." Knowing that he was dying, Hay bravely added "had" interlinearly—Hay's 1905 Diary, Hay Papers, Library of Congress, Washington, D.C.

Chapter Three

1. *Letters of Adams (1892 - 1918)*, p. 120; Stevenson, *Adams*, pp. 52 - 54.

2. For social details, see *Letters of Mrs. Adams*, pp. 235 - 75 *passim; Letters of Adams (1892 - 1918)*, pp. 190, 367, 403n; Cater, ed., *Adams and His Friends*, p. lxix; Robert A Hume, *Runaway Star: An Appreciation of Henry Adams* (Ithaca, N.Y., 1951), pp. 160 - 61. Herbert W. Bowen, a fellow tea drinker, preferred Hay: "He [Adams] was about the same height and age as Mr. Hay was; but he did not have Mr. Hay's magnetism nor intellectual buoyancy"—*Recollections Diplomatic and Undiplomatic* (New York, 1926), p. 272. For political details, see Herbert Edwards, "Henry Adams: Politician and Statesman," *New England Quarterly*, XXII (March, 1949), 55 - 57; Samuels, *Adams: Major Phase*, pp. 309 - 10; J. C. Levenson, *The Mind and Art of Henry Adams* (Boston, 1957), pp. 290, 295; William Appleton Williams, *The Tragedy of American Diplomacy* (Cleveland and New York, 1959), pp. 34 - 39; Clymer, *Hay*, pp. 87, 101, 103, 109, 125, 133 - 34, 276.

3. *Letters of Adams (1892 - 1918)*, pp. 445, 456n; *Letters of Hay*, III, 330.

4. Samuels, *Adams: Major Phase*, p. 328; Henry Adams, *The Education of Henry Adams*, ed. Ernest Samuels (Boston, 1973), p. 505. Edwards theorizes that once Hay had died Adams feared that no official alive "could effect Adams' great and final project of world statesmanship: to bring the Atlantic powers into a permanent coalition. . . ."—"Adams: Politician and Statesman," p. 58.

5. *Letters of Adams (1858 - 1891)*, pp. 343, 337, 383.

6. Samuels, *Adams: Middle Years*, pp. 102 - 04.

7. *Letters of Adams (1858 - 1891)*, pp. 353, 355, 354. From Baden-Baden on August 9, [1883], Constance Fenimore Woolson wrote Hay guess-

ing that he had written *The Bread-Winners,* partly because of details of its Cleveland setting—Woolson Papers, Hay Collection, Brown. For Adams's *Democracy* and Hay, see Henry Holt, *Garrulities of an Octogenarian Editor: With Other Essays Somewhat Biographical and Autobiographical* (Boston and New York, 1923), pp. 134 - 37; Ernest Samuels, ed., *Democracy and Esther: Two Novels by Henry Adams* (Gloucester, Mass., 1965), pp. xi - xiii, xvii.

8. *Letters of Adams (1858 - 1891),* p. 403; *Letters of Adams (1892 - 1918),* pp. 44, 453; *Education of Adams,* p. 325.

9. Stevenson, *Adams,* p. 337. Samuels, in *Adams: Major Phase,* p. 401, adds that Adams found Hay's letters a better record of the times than his own *Education.*

10. *Letters of Adams (1892 - 1918),* p. 474; see also *Adams and His Friends,* p. 590.

11. *Letters of Hay,* II, 269. Hay was writing about Wayne MacVeagh and Rome—identification courtesy of Key, Hay Papers, Library of Congress, which also sheds light as follows on the unbelievable shower of initials in *Letters of Hay,* III, 152: Choate, Pauncefote, Salisbury, Tower, Salisbury, Sun, Miles, Beef Court, Armour, Alger, Miles, Eliot, Leiter, Nancy, Semla, and Curzon. Samuels, in *Adams: Major Phase,* p. 404, having collated Hay's originals and Clara's authorized version, brands the resulting edition "indescribably grotesque"; see also pp. 400 - 01.

12. Edmund Wilson, *The Shock of Recognition: The Development of Literature in the United States Recorded by the Men Who Made It* (Garden City, N.Y., 1943), p. 744.

13. *Letters of Adams (1892 - 1918),* pp. 301, 303.

14. *Mark Twain - Howells Letters: The Correspondence of Samuel L. Clemens and William D. Howells 1872 - 1910,* ed. Henry Nash Smith and William M. Gibson (Cambridge, Mass., 1960), p. 55; Albert Bigelow Paine, *Mark Twain: A Biography: The Personal and Literary Life of Samuel Langhorne Clemens* (New York, 1912), pp. 1249 - 50. I quote from Twain by permission of Thomas G. Chamberlain and Manufacturers Hanover Trust Company as trustees under the Will of Clara Clemens Samossoud.

15. Kenton J. Clymer, "John Hay and Mark Twain," *Missouri Historical Review,* LXXVII (April, 1973), 399; Paine, *Twain,* p. 1249. See also *ibid.,* pp. 308 - 24 *passim;* Thayer, Life of Hay, I, 245 - 80 *passim.*

16. Hay to Twain, January 9, 1871, Mark Twain Papers, University of California, Berkeley. See also Samuel L. Clemens, "John Hay and the Ballads," *Harper's Weekly,* XLIX (October 21, 1905), 1530; Joseph Bucklin Bishop, "A Friendship with John Hay," *Century,* LXXI (March, 1906), 773 - 80.

17. Justin Kaplan, *Mr. Clemens and Mark Twain: A Biography* (New York, 1966), p. 167; Bryant Morley French, *Mark Twain and The Gilded Age: The Book That Named an Era* (Dallas, 1965), pp. 11 - 13.

18. *Twain-Howells Letters,* pp. 55, 56.

19. Paine, *Twain*, p. 533; *Twain-Howells Letters*, p. 277. Clara Hay may have regarded Twain as too unorthodox. See *ibid.*, p. 23; *Mark Twain's Autobiography*, ed. Albert Bigelow Paine (New York and London, 1924), I, 233 - 34; *Mark Twain to Mrs. Fairbanks*, ed. Dixon Wecter (San Marino, Calif., 1949), pp. 186 - 87; Clymer, *Hay*, p. 9.

20. *Twain-Howells Letters*, p. 274; see also Paine, *Twain*, pp. 652 - 53.

21. *Twain-Howells Letters*, pp. 308 - 11; *Letters of Hay*, II, 45.

22. Dennett, *Hay*, p. 103; *Twain-Howells Letters*, p. 271.

23. *Mark Twain in Eruption: Hitherto Unpublished Pages about Men and Events* (New York and London, 1940), pp. 203 - 04. See also Paine, *Twain*, p. 580; Albert Bigelow Paine, ed., *Mark Twain's Notebook* (New York and London, 1935), p. x. The best collection of editions of "1601" is in the Hay Collection, Brown.

24. *Twain-Howells Letters*, pp. 431 - 32.

25. *Twain to Mrs. Fairbanks*, ed., Wecter, p. 256.

26. *Mark Twain's Letters*, ed. Albert Bigelow Paine (New York and London, 1917), II, 761 - 62. Clymer, in "Hay and Twain," pp. 403 - 05, attributes the diminution of the Hay-Twain friendship to fundamental political differences.

27. *Letters of Hay*, II, 7, 11.

28. William Dean Howells, *Life in Letters of William Dean Howells*, ed. Mildred Howells (Garden City, N.Y., 1928), I, 279, 288 - 89. Howells thought that Hay would try for Congress from Ohio—*Twain-Howells Letters*, p. 272.

29. *Life in Letters of Howells*, I, 311; *Letters of Hay*, II, 71.

30. *Life in Letters of Howells*, I, 316, 319, 337, 357 - 58.

31. *Letters of Hay*, II, 184 - 85, 192; *Life in Letters of Howells*, II, 4 - 5; Clara Kirk, *William Dean Howells and Art in His Time* (New Brunswick, N.J., 1965), p. 260.

32. Van Wyck Brooks, *Howells: His Life and World* (New York, 1959), pp. 284n, 242 - 43; see Hay, *Castilian Days*, pp. 122 - 23, 133, 150 - 52.

33. Monteiro, *James and Hay*, pp. 6 - 7.

34. Ilse Dusoir Lind, "The Inadequate Vulgarity of Henry James," *PMLA*, LXVI (December, 1951), 886 - 910; Leon Edel and Ilse Dusoir Lind, eds., Henry James, *Parisian Sketches: Letters to the* New York Tribune *1875 - 1876* (New York, 1957), pp. xii - xxiii, 209 - 15 *passim;* Monteiro, *James and Hay*, pp. 12 - 16.

35. Monteiro, *James and Hay*, pp. 22, 23; *Letters of Hay*, II, 74.

36. Monteiro, *James and Hay*, p. 23.

37. *Ibid.*, pp. 25, 29 - 30; Leon Edel, *Henry James: The Middle Years: 1882 - 1895* (Philadelphia and New York, 1962), pp. 357 - 62; Rayburn S. Moore, *Constance Fenimore Woolson* (New York, 1963), p. 38.

38. *Letters of Hay*, III, 84.

39. *The Letters of Henry James*, ed. Percy Lubbock (New York, 1920), I, 264; Leon Edel, *Henry James: The Treacherous Years: 1895 - 1901*

(Philadelphia and New York, 1969), pp. 232 - 39; Homans, *Education*, pp. 85 - 98 *passim.*

40. *Letters of Adams (1892 - 1918)*, p. 333n; *Letters of Hay*, III, 260. Edel, *James: Treacherous Years*, p. 234, opines that in *The Sacred Fount* the hefty heroine's vampirism of her tired husband may relate to Mrs. Cameron and Adams. But why not theorize that Clara Hay was draining her husband? After all, Hay had been a Cleveland Vampire Club member, perhaps to his wife's annoyance.

41. *The Letters of Theodore Roosevelt*, ed. Elting E. Morison (Cambridge, Mass., 1951 - 1954), I, 390, VI, 1490.

42. Monteiro, *James and Hay*, pp. 37 - 38, 135; Edel, *James: Treacherous Years*, p. 236. James probably never knew that Hay was the author of the *The Bread-Winners*.

43. Nicolay's daughter Helen Nicolay wrote a biography of her father entitled *Lincoln's Secretary: A Biography of John G. Nicolay* (New York, 1949), which recalls many anecdotes involving their treasured friend Colonel Hay. Mather's son Amasa Stone Mather wrote respectfully of Uncle John Hay—see *Extracts from the Letters Diary and Notebooks of Amasa Stone Mather: June 1907 to December 1908* (Cleveland, 1910), I, 50, 117, 272. Miss Woolson's letters to Hay, in which she reaches out for some gesture of platonic regard, are almost unbearably poignant—see Woolson Papers, Hay Collection, Brown.

44. Horace Traubel, *With Walt Whitman in Camden* (Philadelphia, 1953; Carbondale, Ill., 1959), IV, 31 - 32. See also William E. Barton, *Abraham Lincoln and Walt Whitman* (Indianapolis, 1928), pp. 69, 70, 79; Alvin H. Rosenfeld, "Whitman and the Providence Literati," *Books at Brown*, XXIV (1971), 93 - 100 *passim.* Whitman was the first American writer named by Hay in *Castilian Days* (see p. 18); he mentions Whitman twice in his *Addresses* (see pp. 67, 90). Nicolay and Hay quote from *Song of Myself* in their *Lincoln* (see I, 233n).

Chapter Four

1. Clarence Hay, "Introduction" to *The Complete Poetical Works of John Hay* (Boston and New York, 1916), p. xiv. This edition reprints Hay's 1890 collection and adds "Uncollected Pieces." Subsequent page references will be to this edition and will be made parenthetically in the text and footnotes.

2. Sister Saint Ignatius Ward, *The Poetry of John Hay* (Washington, 1930), pp. 51 - 54.

3. Thayer, *Life of Hay*, I, 373, 375 - 76, 355.

4. Hay, in *Castilian Days*, p. 280, contrasts the profane Western idiom "passed in his checks" with the Spanish "gone to give an account of his masses."

5. Compare "With a nigger squat on her safety-valve"—Hay, "Jim Bludso" (p. 4), 1871—with "nigger roosting on the safety-valve!"—Mark

Twain and Charles Dudley Warner, *The Gilded Age: A Tale of To-day*, 1873, *Writings of Twain*, X, 50.

6. Ward, *Poetry of Hay*, table opp. p. 28.

7. Earl Daniels, *The Art of Reading Poetry* (New York, 1941), pp. 88 - 92. Curiously, Whitelaw Reid claimed credit for suggesting the final stanza of "Jim Bludso"—as well as that of "Little Breeches"—see Thayer, *Life of Hay*, I, 371 - 72n.

8. Ward, *Poetry of Hay*, p. 49.

9. Dennett, *Hay*, pp. 78, 79. Twenty-one years after "Little Breeches" first appeared, Benjamin Butler quoted it disapprovingly and criticized its message—see *Autobiography and Personal Reminiscences of Major-General Benjamin F. Butler: Butler's Book: A Review of His Legal, Political, and Military Career* (Boston, 1892), p. 264.

10. Ward, *Poetry of Hay*, p. 44.

11. For Hay's opinion of Doña Isabel, see *Castilian Days*, p. 413.

12. In real life, Hay's King Salomon was evidently old Salomon (1051 - c.1087), King of Hungary from 1063 until Geza I defeated him in 1074 at Mogyorod.

13. "The union of crozier and sceptre had been, if anything, too successful in [Spain]," Hay says, in *Castilian Days*, p. 61. See also p. 211. On p. 292 Hay adds that Spain has been cursed by "crown, crozier, and sabre."

14. Hay seems to have a small-foot fixation—see *Castilian Days*, p. 10, and a few additional poetic lines quoted in the text below.

15. Ward, *Poetry of Hay*, table opp. p. 28.

16. Howells, "Hay in Literature," p. 344.

17. "The Enchanted Shirt" proved to be so popular that it was issued in book form (New York and Chicago, 1889) touchingly illustrated by James Sinclair and printed with refreshing simplicity.

18. This poem mentions the Jacqueminot, then a rare type of rose, also featured in *The Bread-Winners*, p. 105. Readers might have linked Hay and the anonymous novelist through this similarity, among others. For another example, Hay's poem "A Dream of Bric-a-Brac" mentions netsukes (p. 100) as does the novel (p. 126).

19. "Perhaps the conclusion is a little weak . . ."—*Letters of Adams (1858 - 1891)*, p. 383.

20. "I knew a hoydenish little gypsy who bore the tearful name of Lagrimas," reports Hay in *Castilian Days*, p. 36.

21. For a terse prose account of the same incident, see Nicolay and Hay, *Lincoln*, IX, 232.

22. For Hay's earlier, similar comments on Paestum, see *Castilian Days*, pp. 202 - 03.

Chapter Five

1. *Castilian Days*, p. 61. See also pp. 212, 292. Subsequent references to this work will be made parenthetically in the text.

2. Dennett, *Hay*, p. 82. Hay had become more tolerant of Catholics by
the time he and Nicolay wrote *Lincoln*, I, 235.

3. Like most American travel writers, Hay is confused on the subject of
tradition. He criticizes Madrid for lacking it and later approves when a
Spaniard praises America for lacking it. For a fine, brief discussion of tradition and American travel writers, see James L. Dean, *Howells' Travels
toward Art* (Albuquerque, N.M., 1970), pp. 5 - 6.

4. Spanish Charles I was Holy Roman Emperor Charles V. Since
Castilian Days concerns Spain, Charles V is regularly called here by his
Spanish title.

5. Earlier in his life, Hay was more sympathetic toward spiritualism—see *Poet in Exile*, p. 43. He also makes serious use of a spiritualist
in his 1871 short story "The Blood Seedling." But later he ridicules Bott the
spiritualist in *The Bread-Winners*.

6. For Lieutenant-General Don Juan Prim in Mexico, 1861 - 1862, see
Nicolay and Hay, *Lincoln*, VI, 39 - 45 *passim*.

7. Hay sensibly deplores dueling here; yet in *Lincoln*, II, 54 - 55, he
and Nicolay praise Anson Burlingame's acceptance of Preston S. Brooks's
challenge, following the latter's attack on Charles Sumner in the U.S.
Senate.

8. In *Lincoln*, V, 395, 398, General Stonewall Jackson and Philip II are
compared because of their almost identically expressed gratitude to God
rather than to fellow mortals for military success.

9. Royall Tyler, in *Spain: A Study of Her Life and Arts* (London, 1913),
p. 223, calls the Escorial "not unworthy to be ranked as the eighth marvel
of the world," and adds that it was not intended to look like the gridiron on
which St. Lawrence was martyred.

10. Albert F. Calvert and C. Gasquoine Hartley, in *The Prado: A
Description of the Principal Pictures in the Madrid Gallery* (London, 1907),
p. 1, say of the Prado that ". . . a special character . . . places it alone
among the art collections of Europe, and gives it so singular a distinction.
Often it has been called a congress of masterpieces."

11. For more detailed anti-Tyler commentary, see Nicolay and Hay, *Lincoln*, I, 224, III, 150 - 52, 165 - 68.

12. In *The Bread-Winners*, p. 181, Hay awkwardly describes "maidens
of less pretensions."

13. In his review of *Castilian Days*, Howells expressed his pleasure at
finding "a man as well as an author" there; *Atlantic Monthly*, XXVIII
(November, 1871), 637.

Chapter Six

1. The Adee-Hay piece is "The Life-Magnet," *Putnam's Magazine*, VI
(August, 1870), 152 - 62. Monteiro in "Hay's Short Fiction," p. 544n, calls it
a "Poesque tale of metempsychosis, madness, and experimental science."

2. "Red, White, and Blue," *Harper's Weekly*, V (October 19, 1861), 667. Subsequent citations will be made parenthetically in the text.

3. The story is unsigned, but Thayer, *Life of Hay*, I, 354, attributes it to Hay, as does Monteiro, in "Hay's Short Fiction," p. 544. Hay undoubtedly knew Lincoln's secretary of the navy Gideon Welles's wife Mary Jane Welles in Washington, D.C., in 1861; perhaps her name inspired Hay to call the waltz-party hostess Mrs. Welles in his story.

4. For discussions of such diplomats, see Nicolay and Hay, *Lincoln*, VII, 409, 412 - 13, VIII, 267 - 80 *passim*.

5. Monteiro, "Hay's Short Fiction," p. 545.

6. John Hay, "Shelby Cabell," *Harper's New Monthly Magazine*, XXXIII (October, 1866), 607. Brinton's first name, Lorthrop, is given in "Kane and Abel," a later story by Hay in which he figures more prominently.

7. John Hay, "The Foster-Brothers," *Harper's New Monthly Magazine*, XXXIX (September, 1869), 539. Subsequent citations will be made parenthetically in the text.

8. Monteiro, "Hay's Short Fiction," pp. 546, 548.

9. *Ibid.*, pp. 550, 551.

10. *Ibid.*, p. 548n.

11. *Ibid.*, p. 549.

12. Vandersee, ed., *The Bread-Winners*, pp. 18 - 19, 53.

13. Hay, *The Bread-Winners*, ed. Vandersee, p. 59. Subsequent citations will be made parenthetically in the text and footnotes. For background, see Jaher, "Industrialism and the American Aristocrat," pp. 73 - 74. For an adverse opinion of Hay's anti labor position, see Granville Hicks, "The Conversion of John Hay," *New Republic*, LXVII (June 10, 1931), 100 - 01.

14. For the strike background, see Jaher, "Industrialism and the American Aristocrat," pp. 70 - 73.

15. Vandersee, ed., *Bread-Winners*, annotates this name—see p. 124n—and other biblical material in the novel, much of it curiously irrelevant to Hay's evident purposes.

16. Jaher, "Industrialism and the American Aristocrat," p. 91, suggests that Temple's characterization is "softened" because of Hay's "roots and . . . ties to western entrepreneurship."

17. This sequence caused much contemporary response—see Vandersee, ed., *Bread-Winners*, p. 153. Even Henry Adams was moved to comment—see *Letters of Adams (1858 - 1891)*, p. 356.

18. Vandersee, ed., *Bread-Winners*, pp. 32 - 33.

19. Vandersee, *ibid.*, p. 46, offers the names of better candidates for such notoriety. Nicolay and Hay, in *Lincoln*, I, 63 - 64, 103 - 04, 183, 292, are highly critical of Jacksonians in Illinois back in the 1820s and 1830s.

20. Jaher, "Industrialism and the American Aristocrat," p. 85, notes "a touch of nostalgia" in Hay's characterization of Saul, "a skilled artisan reminiscent perhaps of the village workmen of Hay's boyhood."

21. Vandersee, ed., *Bread-Winners*, p. 45, notes that Hay is guilty of
self-deception, as well as untruthfulness and careless writing, when he has
Sleeny quickly identify "the laziest workers in town—a town of 200,000
people!" Publicly, Hay later spoke with better balance of "equal justice to
labor and to capital; . . . honest money and the right to earn it"—*Addresses*, p. 273 (see also p. 281).

22. Hay wrongly insisted in his tardy "Prefatory Sketch" that "The hero
of the tale is Offitt, not Farnham" (p. 57). Jaher, "Industrialism and the
American Aristocrat," pp. 87 - 88, also sees autobiographical touches in
Farnham.

23. In these respects, as in others, Hay echoes and also anticipates common themes used by Mark Twain. A *Bale-Fire* question, "Has a carnival of
crime set in amongst us?" (p. 266), rings changes on Twain's title "The
Facts Concerning the Recent Carnival of Crime in Connecticut" (1876).
On the same page, Hay scoffs at the proposal, advanced in the *Bale-Fire*,
for a public monument to martyred Offitt; perhaps this encouraged
Twain's well-known idea for a monument to Adam. Twain frequently
ridiculed the jury system, best in *The Gilded Age*. Temple's profanity
makes the man seem more like Twain than Hay. Temple was a delight to
1883 - 1884 readers—see Vandersee, ed., *Bread-Winners*, p. 16.

24. Nicolay and Hay, *Lincoln*, IV, 427 - 28, praise Chicago's Irish
Brigade, in action at Lexington, Missouri, early in the Civil War.

25. [John Hay], " 'The Bread-Winners.' A Letter from the Author,"
Century Magazine, XXVII (March, 1884), 795. Hay might legitimately
have added that Richard Watson Gilder, *Century* editor, censored some of
his franker passages—see David E. E. Sloane, "Censoring for *The Century
Magazine:* R. W. Gilder to John Hay on *The Bread-Winners*, 1882 - 1884,"
American Literary Realism, IV (Summer, 1971), 255 - 67.

26. Jaher, "Industrialism and the American Aristocrat," p. 88, notes that
its *objets d'art* resemble those of Henry Adams.

27. Rodney Blake, "How John Hay Suppressed a First Edition," *Biblio*, I
(October, 1921), 77 - 78; Clifford A. Bender, "Another Forgotten Novel,"
Modern Language Notes, XLI (May, 1926), 319 - 22; Vandersee, ed., *Bread-
Winners*, pp. 34 - 36.

28. *Ibid.*, pp. 37 - 38.

29. David E. E. Sloane, "John Hay's *The Bread-Winners* as Literary
Realism," *American Literary Realism*, II (Fall, 1969), 276 - 79.

30. Vandersee, ed., *Bread-Winners*, p. 76n and elsewhere *passim*.

31. Hay effectively uses this rhetorical device elsewhere. For example,
". . . the cedar rafters above you preserve the memory and the odors of
Lebanon"—*Castilian Days*, p. 199.

32. Vandersee, ed., *Bread-Winners*, pp. 20 - 21, touches on this important critical topic. Jaher, "Industrialism and the American Aristocrat," p.
91, notes that the girls' contrasting coloration—Maud is dark; Alice,
fair—conforms to "the iconography of American fiction."

Chapter Seven

1. Thayer, *Life of Hay*, II, 19 - 20, 23 - 24; Blanck, *Bibliography of American Literature*, IV, 45.

2. Nicolay and Hay, *Lincoln*, I, xiv. Subsequent citations will be made parenthetically in the text and footnotes. Victor Searcher, *Lincoln Today: An Introduction to Modern Lincolniana* (New York, 1969) p. 68, reports that according to material in the Nicolay Papers, Library of Congress, Nicolay wrote 224 of the 330 chapters. The statement is erroneous, since *Lincoln* contains only 224 chapters altogether; however, Searcher's proportions may well be correct. In a letter to Francis H. Scott, treasurer of the Century Company, December 30, 1896, in Nicolay Papers, Library of Congress, Nicolay does report that for the projected abridgment of *Lincoln* "Col. Hay and I . ∴ . have worked over in a preliminary way about one-half of the chapters written by each. . . ." Ultimately Nicolay alone did the abridgment, published in 1902.

3. Dennett, *Hay*, p. 137; Paul M. Angle, "Introduction" to his abridged edition of Nicolay and Hay, *Abraham Lincoln: A History* (Chicago, 1966), p. xix.

4. Dennett, *Hay*, pp. 135 - 36; Searcher, *Lincoln Today*, p. 15.

5. For Hay and newspaper sources, see Henry B. Van Hoesen, "John Hay and the Historian's Use of Newspapers," in *Bookmen's Holiday: Notes and Studies Written and Gathered in Tribute of Harry Miller Lydenberg*, ed. Deogh Fulton (New York, 1943), pp. 395 - 98.

6. Not all 128 volumes of the *War of the Rebellion* (Washington, 1880 - 1901) were available to Nicolay and Hay; but they used all three volumes of the *Report of the Joint Committee on the Conduct of the War*, 38th Congress, 2nd Session (Washington, 1865).

7. Sherman praised Hay for his historical work, in a magnificent letter to Hay dated January 31, 1880—see Evelyn W. Symington Papers, Library of Congress.

8. The items by Force and Pond are part of *Campaigns of the Civil War*, 13 vols (New York, 1881 - 1885), most of which Nicolay and Hay consulted. In fact, Nicolay wrote *The Outbreak of the Rebellion*, which was the first volume of the Scribner's Army in the Civil War series, and Hay reviewed several other volumes in it—see George Monteiro, ed., "John Hay and the Union Generals," *Journal of the Illinois State Historical Society*, LXIX (February, 1976), 46 - 66.

9. For a photograph of election statistics in Lincoln's hand, see David Homer Bates, *Lincoln in the Telegraph Office: Recollections of the United States Telegraph Corps during the Civil War* (New York, 1907), opp. p. 278.

10. Unfortunately, *Lincoln* by Nicolay and Hay lacks a bibliography. Moreover, quoted historians and other war commentators are usually not indexed. These omissions make any study of the authors' use of sources difficult and inefficient.

11. Angle, *Shelf of Lincoln Books*, p. 34.

12. Butler, commanding general of the Union forces occupying New Orleans in 1862, reviled Hay's writing here—see *Autobiography of Butler*, pp. 243, 260, 264, 421.

13. Hay probably learned much about Mexico at the time of the Civil War from John Bigelow, his superior officer in the Paris legation—see Bigelow, *Retrospections of an Active Life: Volume III: 1865 - 1866* (New York, 1909), pp. 497 - 500, 662 - 66.

14. Edmund Wilson, in *Patriotic Gore: Studies in the Literature of the American Civil War* (New York, 1962), pp. 104 - 05 discusses Lincoln's meditation well. In his Second Inaugural Address, Lincoln publicly made the same point which is the core of his private meditation (X, 144). In 1902 Hay delivered a moving speech based on Lincoln's meditation—see *Addresses*, pp. 237 - 40.

15. Nicolay and Hay, *Lincoln*, IX, 377, report Lincoln's 212 electoral votes to McClellan's mere twenty-one but neglect to add that Lincoln amassed only 55 percent of the total popular vote. He received only 2,330,-552 votes to McClellan's 1,835,985—see E. B. Long, *The Civil War Day by Day: An Almanac 1861 - 1865* (New York, 1971), p. 594.

16. David Madden writes of "the urge to violence [war] that is the Siamese twin of the American urge to peace and tranquility [good politics]," in *Tough Guy Writers of the Thirties* (Carbondale, Ill., 1968), p. xxix.

17. See Colin R. Ballard, *The Military Genius of Abraham Lincoln: An Essay* (Cleveland, 1952).

18. Hay comments on fate in some of his speeches—see *Addresses*, pp. 14, 205 - 06, 248, 249, 250. For Grant in criticism of the word "if," see *Personal Memoirs of U. S. Grant*, ed. E. B. Long (Cleveland and New York, 1952), pp. 188 - 89; see also pp. 408, 412.

19. Chase once put Lincoln's portrait on high-denomination bank notes and his own on those of lower denomination, "as was becoming," he explained; he once wrote Lincoln that he would see certain matters Chase's way when he was better informed (IX, 395, 398).

20. For other evidence of sarcasm leveled at McClellan, see IV, 470, V, 315, 360, 368, 373 - 74, 379, VI, 142n, 144 - 45, 180, 184.

21. With less excuse, Nicolay and Hay employ this same dodge, hinting at least a score of times that, but for lack of space, they would go into more detail to prove points and extend coverage. Chapters especially loaded with sarcasm are those dealing with the Union army's reverses at Yorktown and the Seven Days—see in particular V, 360, 368, 374, 414, 424, 431 - 32, 438.

22. Hay, however, praises Ohio pioneers thus: "They were loyal to the last drop of their blood, to their consciences, to their families, to their country"; "The Pioneers of Ohio: An Address Delivered before the Pioneers' Association of the Western Reserve, at Burgess' Grove, Cuyahoga County, Ohio, August 27th, 1879," reprinted in *Magazine of History, with Notes and Queries*, XXVI, No. 3, Extra No. 103 (1924), 290.

23. On the unacknowledged use of their work on Lincoln by one later biographer, Hay once wrote Nicolay, "By the way, I would like to say in public some time that Morse, in his 'Lincoln,' reminded me of a burglar, leaving a house with his bag full of plate and stopping to scribble something insulting on the front door, or, you can say it if you like"—*Letters of Hay*, III, 108.

24. The 1894 two-volume edition by Nicolay and Hay of Lincoln's writings reproduces the materials without apparatus. Its value and that of their twelve-volume, briefly annotated 1905 version, which was in reality edited by Francis D. Tandy, therefore lies in its preservation of materials, which might otherwise have been lost. For an indication of the value of Nicolay and Hay in editing Lincoln's writings, see Roy P. Basler, ed., *The Collected Works of Abraham Lincoln*, 12 vols. and Index vol. (New Brunswick, N.J., 1953 - 1955), I, viii, Index vol. pp. 1 - 2, 55, 113 - 14, 203 - 04, 337, 349. See also Angle, *Shelf of Lincoln Books*, pp. 3 - 8. Angle reports that the 1894 edition prints 1,736 Lincoln items; the 1905 edition, only 518 additional ones.

25. The quantity and complexity of twentieth-century scholarship on aspects of the Civil War is incredible. "It has been estimated that over 100,-000 volumes and pamphlets exist relating in some manner or other to the Civil War," say Ralph Newman and E. B. Long in *The Civil War* (New York, 1956), II, 225. It is therefore beyond the scope of this work to attempt to cope with the occasional relationship of even the best of that literature to Nicolay and Hay.

Chapter Eight

1. Hay's contemporary reputation as an orator in England was incredible: ". . . the literary quality of nothing that he wrote was finer than that of the addresses—all too few—which he was called upon to deliver during the year and a half of his service near the Court of St. James's"—Joseph S. Gilder, "John Hay," *The Critic*, XLVII (August, 1905), 113.

2. *Addresses*, p. 282. Subsequent citations will be made parenthetically in the text.

3. See Sol Gittleman, "John Hay as a Critic of *The Rubaiyat of Omar Khayyam*," *Victorian Newsletter*, No. 24 (Fall, 1963), pp. 26 - 27.

4. Meanwhile, Hay privately noted that the Fair was tiring and filled him "with despair"—*Letters of Hay*, III, 296.

5. *Ibid.*, III, 321.

6. The last chapter, "A Decade's Delay," pp. 334 - 48, of *The American 1890s: Life and Times of a Lost Generation* (New York, 1966), by Larzer Ziff, reads like an indictment of much that Hay stood for.

Selected Bibliography

PRIMARY SOURCES

1. *Manuscript Collections*

Most of John Hay's manuscript materials, especially letters and diaries, are in the Reference Department, Manuscript Division, Library of Congress, Washington, D.C.; the John Hay Collection in the Brown University Library, Providence, R.I.; the Houghton Manuscript Library, Harvard University, Cambridge, Mass.; the Massachusetts Historical Society, Boston, Mass.; and the Western Reserve Historical Society, Cleveland, Ohio. The manuscript of *The Bread-Winners* is in the Houghton Library, Harvard. In the Hay Collection at Brown is the compositor's copy of the autographed manuscript of *The Bread-Winners*, believed to be in Hay's handwriting disguised, chapters 1 - 17, with chapters 18 - 20 lacking. Brown also has some manuscript verse. Hay's autograph manuscript of "The Army of the Potomac" (*Abraham Lincoln*, vol. 4, ch. 25) is in the Evelyn W. Symington Papers, Library of Congress. For details as to the location of other manuscript materials, see William Easton Louttit, Jr. (below) and David E. E. Sloane, "John Hay (1838 - 1905)" (below).

2. *Books*

Pike County Ballads and Other Pieces. Boston: Osgood, 1871.

Castilian Days. Boston: Osgood, 1871. Boston and New York: Houghton, Mifflin, rev. ed., 1890; abridged ed., 1903.

Amasa Stone: Born April 27, 1818 Died May 11, 1883. New York: Devinne [1883].

The Bread-Winners: A Social Study. New York: Harper, 1884; rev. ed., 1893; with anon. "Prefatory Sketch" [by Hay], 1899; with "Introduction" by Clarence Hay, 1916. Ridgewood, N.J.: Gregg, 1967, facsimile reprint of 1884 ed. New Haven: College & University, 1973, ed. Charles Vandersee—the best edition, with superb "Introduction," "Bibliographical Note," "Textual Note," Hay's 1899 "Prefatory Sketch," and Clarence Hay's 1916 "Introduction." Translations include *Die Sozialisten*, Stuttgart: Engelhorn, 1885; *Le Bien D'Autrui: Etude de Moeurs Americaines*, Paris: Hachette, 1886.

Dr. Charles Hay: Born February 7, 1801. Died September 18, 1884. New York: Devinne [1884?].

Poems by John Hay. Boston and New York: Houghton Mifflin, 1890.

Abraham Lincoln: A History. With John G. Nicolay. 10 vols. New York: Century, 1890. Abridged by Nicolay as *A Short Life of Abraham Lin-*

coln, *Condensed from Nicolay & Hay's Abraham Lincoln: A History.*
New York: Century, 1902. Abridged and interpolated by Paul M.
Angle as *Abraham Lincoln: A History.* Chicago: University of
Chicago, 1966.
*Abraham Lincoln, Complete Works: Comprising His Speeches, State
Papers, and Miscellaneous Writings.* 2 vols. New York: Century, 1894.
Ed. by John G. Nicolay and John Hay. Contains 1,736 items and the
text of the Lincoln-Douglas debates. Good work then, but now regard-
ed as quite incomplete and slightly inaccurate textually. Reissued as
Complete Works of Abraham Lincoln. "New and Enlarged Edition."
Ed. John G. Nicolay and John Hay. 12 vols. New York: Tandy, 1905.
Really edited by Francis D. Tandy, who added 518 new items.
Addresses of John Hay. New York: Century, 1906. Reprinted Freeport,
N.Y.: Books for Libraries, 1970.
Letters of John Hay and Extracts from Diary. 3 vols. Washington, D.C.,
1908. Privately printed (by Clara Stone Hay) but not published.
Anonymously edited and with a factual, tender introduction by Henry
Adams. New York: Gordian, 1969, facsimile reprint.
A Poet in Exile: Early Letters of John Hay. Ed. Caroline Ticknor. Boston
and New York: Houghton Mifflin, 1910. A few juvenile letters and
poems, 1858 - 1860, to Nora Perry of Providence, R.I.
The Life and Letters of John Hay. By William Roscoe Thayer. 2 vols.
Boston: Houghton Mifflin, 1915. Contains many letters.
The Complete Poetical Works of John Hay. "Introduction" by Clarence
Hay. Boston and New York: Houghton Mifflin, 1916; with indexes of
first lines and titles, 1917. Reprints the 1890 edition and adds previous-
ly uncollected pieces. New York: AMS, 1970, facsimile reprint. St.
Clair Shores, Mich.: Scholarly, 1970, reprint.
A College Friendship: A Series of Letters from John Hay to Hannah Angell.
Ed. Amy A. C. Montague. Boston: Privately printed, 1938. Romantic,
melancholy letters to a close Providence, R.I., friend, one with whom
he was then (mid-1858 to early 1871) probably in love.
Lincoln and the Civil War in the Diaries and Letters of John Hay. Selected
and with Introduction by Tyler Dennett. New York: Dodd, Mead,
1939. Reprinted Westport, Conn.: Greenwood, 1972. Invaluable
source book, well edited; includes material through 1870. Much of the
material here repeats items in William Roscoe Thayer's *Life and
Letters of John Hay* but is more accurate.

3. *Short Stories*
"Red, White, and Blue," *Harper's Weekly,* V (October 19, 1861), 666 - 67.
"Shelby Cabell," *Harper's Monthly Magazine,* XXXIII (October, 1866),
601 - 11.
"The Foster-Brothers," *Harper's Monthly Magazine,* XXXIX (September,
1869), 535 - 66.

"The Blood Seedling," *Lippincott's Magazine,* VII (March, 1871), 281 - 93.
"Kane and Abel," *Frank Leslie's Illustrated Newspaper,* April 22, 1871, pp. 85 - 87.

4. *Articles (selective)*
"Ellsworth," *Atlantic Monthly,* VIII (July, 1861), 119 - 25. Praises Col. E. E. Ellsworth. Rewritten as "A Young Hero; Personal Reminiscences of Colonel E. E. Ellsworth," *McClure's Magazine,* VI (March, 1896), 354 - 61.
" 'The Bread-Winners.' A Letter from the Author," *Century Magazine,* XXVII (March, 1884), 794 - 96. Comments, cloaked in anonymity, on *The Bread-Winners.*
"Life in the White House in the Time of Lincoln," *Century Magazine,* XLI (November, 1890), 33 - 37.
"The Love of a Nun." *See* W. Easton Louttit, Jr., "The Love of a Nun," *Colophon,* n.s. II, No. 4 (Autumn, 1937), 504 - 10. Prints Hay's synopsis of his projected five-act play *The Love of a Nun,* involving Protestant Henry III of Navarre at Montmartre, a Catholic abbess of Montmartre, and her lover Castignac, an officer with Henry. Dull, slight, operatic. Louttit dates the manuscript between 1876 and 1879.

SECONDARY SOURCES

1. *Bibliographies*
BLANCK, JACOB. "John Milton Hay," in *Bibliography of American Literature,* IV. New Haven and London: Yale University, 1963. Pp. 37 - 63. Meticulous descriptive bibliography of Hay's works, in three sections: primary books, collections of reprinted materials, and books by others but reprinting materials by Hay.
LOUTTIT, WILLIAM EASTON, JR. "A Short List of His Writings," in Tyler Dennett, *John Hay: From Poetry to Politics.* New York: Dodd, Mead, 1933. Pp. 451 - 56. Divided into periodical publications, translations, books, pamphlets, lyrics and hymns, and collected works. The most complete to its date.
SLOANE, DAVID E. E. "John Hay (1838 - 1905)," *American Literary Realism,* III (Spring, 1970), 178 - 88. Definitive bibliographical essay, divided as follows: history of criticism; bibliographies; editions, reprints and published manuscript materials; sequels; manuscript collections; recent critical articles; and areas needing further attention.
_____. "John Hay," pp. 270 - 71, in Noel Polk, "Guide to Dissertations on American Literary Figures, 1870 - 1910: Part One," *American Literary Realism,* VIII (Summer, 1975), 178 - 280. Lists and comments on all five doctoral dissertations on Hay to date.

2. Books

ADAMS, HENRY. *The Education of Henry Adams*. Ed. Ernest Samuels.
Boston: Houghton Mifflin, 1973. This 1918 American classic, ex-
cellently annotated here, frequently lauds Hay.
————. *Letters from Henry Adams (1858 - 1891)*. Ed. Worthington
Chauncey Ford. Boston and New York: Houghton Mifflin, 1930.
Letters from Henry Adams (1892 - 1918). Ed. Worthington Chauncey
Ford. Boston and New York: Houghton Mifflin, 1938. Invaluable for
an understanding of Hay and Adams.
————. *Henry Adams and His Friends: A Collection of His Unpublished
Letters*. Ed. Harold Dean Cater. Boston: Houghton Mifflin, 1947. Also
valuable.
ADAMS, MARIAN. *The Letters of Mrs. Henry Adams (1865 - 1883)*. Ed.
Ward Thoron. Boston: Little, Brown, 1936. Important for an un-
derstanding of Hay's social life.
ANGLE, PAUL M. *A Shelf of Lincoln Books: A Critical, Selective
Bibliography of Lincolniana*. New Brunswick, N.J.: Rutgers Universi-
ty, 1946. Includes a discussion of Hay's Civil War diary, the biography
of Lincoln by Nicolay and Hay, and their editions of Lincoln's
writings.
BAILEY, THOMAS A. *A Diplomatic History of the American People*. 8th ed.
New York: Appleton-Century-Crofts, 1969. Informative and bal-
anced.
BASLER, ROY P. *The Lincoln Legend: A Study in Changing Conceptions*.
Boston and New York: Houghton Mifflin, 1935. Surveys Lincoln
literature; judges the biography of Lincoln by Nicolay and Hay to be
invaluable as a source book but lacking in unity as a biography.
BEMIS, SAMUEL FLAGG. *A Diplomatic History of the United States*. 3rd ed.
New York: Holt, 1950. Contains praise of Hay.
BISHOP, JOSEPH BUCKLIN. *Notes and Anecdotes of Many Years*. New York:
Scribner's, 1925. Sketches Hay as journalist, editor, and revered friend.
BULLARD, F. LAURISTON. *Abraham Lincoln and the Widow Bixby*. New
Brunswick, N.J.: Rutgers University, 1946. Concludes (pp. 63 - 105
passim) that, contrary to many published rumors, Lincoln and not Hay
wrote the famous letter.
CARTER, EVERETT. *Howells and the Age of Realism*. Philadelphia and New
York: Lippincott, 1954. Reprinted Hamden, Conn.: Archon Books,
1966. Places *The Bread-Winners* in the early tradition of antilabor
novels; analyzes its stereotyped contrasts.
CLEMENS, SAMUEL LANGHORNE. *See* TWAIN, MARK.
CLYMER, KENTON J. *John Hay: The Gentleman as Diplomat*. Ann Arbor:
University of Michigan, 1975. Traces the development of Hay's
thoughts on socio-political matters, race, and international problems

1865 - 1897; then exhaustively treats Hay and Spain, the Philippines, China, England, Alaska, and Panama 1898 - 1905; thoroughly documented.

COLE, WAYNE S. *An Interpretive History of American Foreign Relations.* Homewood, Ill.: Dorsey, 1968. Sees Hay as elitist, imperialistic, and anglophilic.

CORTISSOZ, ROYAL. *The Life of Whitelaw Reid.* 2 vols. New York: Scribner's, 1921. Valuable source of information on the personal and professional friendship of Hay and Reid.

DENNETT, TYLER. *John Hay: From Poetry to Politics.* New York: Dodd, Mead, 1933. Best biography of Hay; stresses politics.

DENNIS, A. L. P. "John Hay," in *The American Secretaries of State and Their Diplomacy.* 10 vols. bound as 5. New York: Knopf, 1928. Reprinted New York: Pageant, 1958. IX, 115 - 89. Praises Hay highly but from a conservative point of view.

Diplomatic History of the Panama Canal: Correspondence Relating to the Negotiation and Application of Certain Treaties on the Subject of the Construction of an Interoceanic Canal, and Accompanying Papers. Washington, D.C., 1914. Includes Hay's pertinent letters and telegrams, and prints all relevant treaties and conventions.

EDEL, LEON. *Henry James: The Middle Years: 1882 - 1895.* Philadelphia and New York: Lippincott, 1962. *Henry James: The Treacherous Years: 1895 - 1901.* Philadelphia and New York: Lippincott, 1969. *Henry James: The Master: 1901 - 1916.* Philadelphia and New York: Lippincott, 1972. All shed light on James's friendship with Hay.

————— and ILSE DUSOIR LIND, eds. Henry James, *Parisian Sketches: Letters to the* New York Tribune *1875 - 1876.* New York: New York University, 1957. Shows the part Hay played in James's obtaining the *Tribune* contract.

EGGLESTON, GEORGE CARY. *Recollections of a Varied Life.* New York: Holt, 1910. Includes reminiscences about Hay by a casual friend.

FERRELL, ROBERT H. *American Diplomacy: A History.* Rev. and expanded. New York: Norton, 1969. Admirably factual.

HERTZ, EMANUEL. *The Hidden Lincoln: From the Letters and Papers of William H. Herndon.* New York: Viking, 1938. Contains Herndon letters to Jesse W. Weik criticizing Nicolay and Hay for their fear of displeasing Robert T. Lincoln, their suppression of material facts, their inclusion of unimportant and irrelevant trivia, and their occasional erroneous conclusions concerning Lincoln.

HOWELLS, WILLIAM DEAN. *Life in Letters of William Dean Howells.* Ed. Mildred Howells. 2 vols. Garden City, N.Y.: Doubleday, Doran [1928]. Reveals details of Howells's friendship with Hay.

JUSSERAND, J. J. *What Me Befell: The Reminicences of J. J. Jusserand.*

Boston and New York: Houghton Mifflin, 1933. Contains praise of and anecdotes concerning Hay by the distinguished French literary critic and diplomat.

KENNAN, GEORGE F. *American Diplomacy: 1900 - 1950*. Chicago: University of Chicago, 1951. Criticizes the adverse effects of the Open Door Policy on American diplomacy.

KOHLSAAT, H. H. *From McKinley to Harding: Personal Recollections of Our Presidents*. New York and London: Scribner's, 1923. Egocentric and chatty, but occasionally informative regarding Hay.

The Life and Works of John Hay 1838 - 1905: A Commemorative Catalogue of the Exhibition Shown at the John Hay Library of Brown University in Honor of the Centennial of His Graduation at the Commencement of 1858. Providence, R.I.: Brown University Library, 1961. Illustrated description of a fine exhibition.

MARDEN, ORISON SWETT. *Talks with Great Workers*. New York: Crowell, 1901. Chapter XXIII, entitled "He Was Equal to His Great Opportunity," pp. 133 - 38, concerns Hay and reveals his authorship of *The Bread-Winners*.

MONTEIRO, GEORGE. *Henry James and John Hay: The Record of a Friendship*. Providence, R.I.: Brown University, 1965. Definitive account.

NEVINS, ALLAN. *Henry White: Thirty Years of American Diplomacy*. New York and London: Harper, 1930. Contains valuable information on Hay's friendship with this superb diplomat and public servant; useful also for historical background.

NICOLAY, HELEN. *Lincoln's Secretary: A Biography of John G. Nicolay*. New York: Longsman, Green, 1949. Vividly evokes images of Hay's human side and reconstructs the process of the writing of Lincoln's biography by Nicolay (the author's father) and Hay.

PARRINGTON, VERNON LOUIS. *Main Currents in American Thought: An Interpretation of American Literature from the Beginnings to 1920.* 3 vols. New York: Harcourt, Brace, 1927, 1930. Contains violent denunciation of *The Bread-Winners* and Hay for alleged antilabor sentiments (III, 171 - 79 *passim*).

REA, GEORGE BRONSON. *What Americans Don't Know about "The Open Door."* Shanghai, June, 1932. Prophetic pro-Japanese criticism of Hay's policy; issued in pamphlet form by the Japanese Association of China.

SAMUELS, ERNEST. *The Young Henry Adams*. Cambridge, Mass.: Harvard University, 1948. *Henry Adams: The Middle Years*. Cambridge, Mass.: Harvard University, 1958. *Henry Adams: The Major Phase*. Cambridge, Mass.: Harvard University, 1964. Provide details of Adams's friendship with Hay.

SEARS, LORENZO. *John Hay: Author and Statesman*. New York: Dodd,

Mead, 1914. Brief biography of limited value; opinionated, fulsome in praise, naïvely jingoistic, and marred by antidemocratic and anti-American prejudices.

THAYER, WILLIAM ROSCOE. *The Life and Letters of John Hay.* 2 vols. Boston: Houghton Mifflin, 1915. Long the standard biography; strengthened by inclusion of innumerable letters but weakened by prejudices.

THURMAN, KELLY. *John Hay as a Man of Letters.* Reseda, California: Mohave Books, 1974. Too brief and general to be very useful.

TWAIN, MARK. *Mark Twain in Eruption: Hitherto Unpublished Pages about Men and Events.* Ed. Bernard DeVoto. New York and London: Harper, 1940. Tells about Hay's response to Twain's "1601."

———— and WILLIAM DEAN HOWELLS. *Mark Twain - Howells Letters: The Correspondence of Samuel L. Clemens and William D. Howells 1872 - 1910.* Ed. Henry Nash Smith and William M. Gibson, with Frederick Anderson. 2 vols., continuously paged. Cambridge, Mass.: Harvard University, 1960. Contains numerous references to Hay.

WARD, SISTER SAINT IGNATIUS. *The Poetry of John Hay.* Washington, D.C.: Catholic University of America, 1930. Pedestrian treatment.

3. *Articles (selective)*

ADAMS, BROOKS. "John Hay," *McClure's Magazine,* XIX (June, 1902), 173 - 82. Extols Hay's diplomatic brilliance and his unselfishness.

BENDER, CLIFFORD A. "Another Forgotten Novel," *Modern Language Notes,* XLI (May, 1926), 319 - 22. Reveals Hay's attitudes toward Henry F. Keenan's novel *The Money-Makers,* 1885, written as an anti-capitalistic reply to Hay's *Bread-Winners;* points out that Keenan's villain was modeled by Hay's father-in-law Amasa Stone.

BLAKE, RODNEY. "How John Hay Suppressed a First Edition," *Biblio,* I (October, 1921), 77 - 78. Summarizes the lengths to which Hay allegedly went to buy up and otherwise suppress Henry F. Keenan's *Money-Makers* (1885).

CHAPMAN, A. A. "The Boyhood of John Hay," *Century Magazine,* LXXVIII (June, 1909), 444 - 54. Pleasant sketch of Hay's boyhood in Warsaw, Illinois.

CLYMER, KENTON J. "John Hay and Mark Twain," *Missouri Historical Review,* LXXVIII (April, 1973), 397 - 406. Thorough review of the evidence of their friendship, with stress on their political differences; nicely illustrated.

DICKASON, DAVID H. "Henry Adams and Clarence King: The Record of a Friendship," *New England Quarterly,* XVII (June, 1944), 229 - 54. Definitive treatment of this friendship; Hay is occasionally mentioned and is related to the subjects.

EDWARDS, HERBERT. "Henry Adams: Politician and Statesman," *New*

England Quarterly, XXII (March, 1949), 49 - 60. Includes a splendid analysis of Adams's influence on Hay's political and diplomatic thinking.

GILDER, JOSEPH B. "John Hay," *Critic*, XLVII (August, 1905), 112 - 13. Standard eulogy; especially praises Hay's 1897 - 1898 public addresses and personal letters.

———. "Glimpses of John Hay," *Critic*, XLVII (September, 1905), 248 - 52. Pleasant, trivial anecdotes about Hay, together with some of his allegedly *bons mots*.

HICKS, GRANVILLE. "The Conversion of John Hay," *New Republic*, LXVII (June 10, 1931), 100 - 01. Criticizes Hay for antilabor prejudice in *The Bread-Winners*.

HOWELLS, WILLIAM DEAN. Review of *Abraham Lincoln: A History*, by John G. Nicolay and John Hay, *Harper's Monthly Magazine*, LXXXII (February, 1891), 478 - 82. Highly praises the style of the joint authors, their tolerance, and their overall fairness.

———. Review of *The Bread-Winners*, *Century Magazine*, XXVIII (May, 1884), 153 - 54. Generally laudatory though signed only "W."

———. "John Hay in Literature," *North American Review*, CLXXXI (September, 1905), 343 - 51. Surveys Hay's literary production.

JAHER, FREDERIC COPLE. "Industrialism and the American Aristocrat: A Social Study of John Hay and His Novel, *The Bread-Winners*," *Journal of the Illinois State Historical Society*, LXV (1972), 69 - 93. Highly valuable, especially on Hay's paradoxically simultaneous praise of aristocracy-culture-taste-inheritance   and   also   pioneering-power-wealth-entrepreneurism; excellently illustrated.

MONTEIRO, GEORGE. "William Dean Howells and *The Breadwinners*," *Studies in Bibliography*, XV (1962), 267 - 68. Presents proof that Howells wrote the prudent, unsigned review of Hay's novel in *Century Magazine*, XXVIII (May, 1884), 153 - 54.

———. "John Hay as Reporter: Special Correspondence on the Great Chicago Fire," *Books at Brown*, XXII (1968), 81 - 94. Thorough account of Hay's coverage of the 1871 Chicago fire.

———. "John Hay's Short Fiction," *Studies in Short Fiction*, VIII (Fall, 1971), 543 - 52. Distinguished critical analysis of Hay's five short stories.

———, ed. "John Hay and the Union Generals," *Journal of the Illinois State Historical Society*, LXIX (February, 1976), 46 - 66. Presents evidence for attributing to Hay six unsigned reviews of military histories of the Civil War appearing late in 1881 and early in 1882 in the New York *Tribune*; reprints the reviews, together with splendid illustrations.

ROSENFELD, ALVIN. "Whitman and the Providence Literati," *Books at Brown*, XXIV (1971), 82 - 103. Treats Hay's relationship with Walt Whitman.

SEARS, LOUIS MARTIN. "John Hay in London, 1897 - 1898," *Ohio Historical Quarterly*, XLV (October, 1956), 356 - 75. Detailed narrative of Hay's ambassadorship, giving Hay high praise, especially for his notable part in handling diplomatic problems involving European powers during the Spanish-American War.

SLOANE, DAVID E. E. "John Hay's *The Bread-Winners* as Literary Realism," *American Literary Realism*, II (Fall, 1969), 276 - 79. Defends caricature, melodrama, and sentimentality in Hay's novel; praises its interlocking plot elements, foreshadowing, and accurate depiction of contemporary social and political motivation.

————. "Censoring for *The Century Magazine:* R. W. Gilder to John Hay on *The Bread-Winners*, 1882 - 1884," *American Literary Realism*, IV (Summer, 1971), 255 - 67. Publishes two letters from Gilder to Hay about Hay's novel and one letter from Gilder's *Century* reader about it; discusses the effects of Gilder's deletions of realistic sexual passages from it.

TAYLOR, GORDON O. "Of Adams and Aquarius," *American Literature*, XLVI (March, 1974), 68 - 82. Includes a contrast of Hay and Henry Adams, as briefly developed by Norman Mailer in his *Armies of the Night* (1968).

THAYER, WILLIAM ROSCOE. "John Hay's Policy of Anglo-Saxonism," *World's Work*, XXXV (November, 1917), 33 - 41. Praises Hay for democratic idealism, Anglo-Saxonism, love of England, premonitions of the rise of militaristic Germany, and diplomatic astuteness; disfigured by bias against the Democratic party and the Irish, and by a propagandistic tone.

VANDERSEE, CHARLES. "The Great Literary Mystery of the Gilded Age," *American Literary Realism*, VII (Summer, 1974), 245 - 72. A long chronological review of unsuccessful contemporary detective work to try to identify the author of *The Bread-Winners*.

Index

(Works by Hay are listed under his name)

Stone, Clara Louise. *See* Hay, Clara Louise Stone
Stone, Flora. *See* Mather, Flora Stone
Stone, Julia Gleason, 21, 92
Sumner, Charles, 19, 99, 140n7
Swedenborg, Emanuel, 85

Takahira, Baron Kogoro, 39, 134 - 35n44
Tandy, Francis D., 145n24
Tarbell, Ida M., 118
Taylor, Bayard, 21, 122
Templeton, Faith, 93; *Drafted In*, 93
Teniers, David, 70
Thirteenth Amendment, The, 104
Thomas Aquinas, St., 44
Thomas, Benjamin P., 118
Thomas, George H., 101, 107, 110
Thomas, Philip F., 100
Tiepolo, Giovanni Battista, 76
Tilden, Samuel J., 23
Titian, 70, 72, 75, 77, 79; *Charles I*, 77
Tolstoy, Count Leo, 123
Topete y Carballo, Juan Bautista, 71
Tourgée, Albion W., 84, 86; *A Royal Gentleman*, 84
Transylvania University, 16
Tucker, George F., 96
Tutuila, 33
Twain, Mark, 15, 21, 41, 45 - 47, 53, 54, 55, 56, 65, 73, 83, 84, 86, 125, 137n19, 137n23, 137n26, 138 - 39n5, 142n23; *Adventures of Huckleberry Finn*, 55, 65; *The Adventures of Tom Sawyer*, 65; "The Babies," 46; "The Facts Concerning the Recent Carnival of Crime in Connecticut," 142n23; *The Gilded Age* (with Charles Dudley Warner), 45, 56, 138 - 39n5, 142n23; *Life on the Mississippi*, 46; "Old Times on the Mississippi," 45 - 46, *Pudd'nhead Wilson*, 84; "1601," 46, 137n23
Twichell, Joseph H., 46, 47
Tyler, John, 79, 85

Valera y Alcalá Galiano, Juan, 71

Vallandigham, Clement L., 103, 116
Vampire Club, The, 22, 46, 92, 138n40
Vandersee, Charles, 87
Van Dyck, Sir Anthony, 70, 79; *Crowning with Thorns*, 79
Velazquez, Diego Rodriguez De Silva y, 70, 73, 74, 75, 76, 77, 78; *Los Borrachos*, 75; *Las Meninas*, 75; *The Surrender of Breda*, 75
Venezuela, 37
Veronese, Paolo, 70, 75
Victoria, Queen (England), 30, 33
Virgil, 123

Wade-Davis Manifesto, 96
Wade-Mason Bill, 104
Walpole, Spencer, 96
War of the Rebellion . . . , 97
Ward, Artemus, 80
Ward, Sister Saint Ignatius, 54, 60
Warden, Robert B., 98
Warner, Charles Dudley, 45, 138 - 39n5; *See also* Twain, Mark, *The Gilded Age*
Welles, Gideon, 97, 106, 141n3; *Diary*, 97
Welles, Mary Janes (Mrs. Gideon), 141n3
Westminster Abbey, 121
White, Henry, 32, 44
Whitman, Sarah, 17
Whitman, Walt, 53, 64, 123, 125, 138n44; *Song of Myself*, 138n44
Whitney, Helen Hay, 22, 28, 40, 48
Wilson, Edmund, 44
Wind and the Lion, The, 134n43
Woolson, Constance Fenimore, 51, 52, 135 - 36n7, 138n43
Wordsworth, William, 64

Ximenez de Cisneros, Cardinal, 72

Yale University, 22, 36

Zola, Emile, 91
Zurbarán, Francesco de, 76

DATE DUE

DEMCO 38-297